the One
revealed

A Woman's Hopeful and Helpful Guide
in Knowing Who Her Husband Is

Copyright

"The One" Revealed: A Woman's Hopeful and Helpful Guide in Knowing Who Her Husband Is

ISBN: 978-0-692-50419-2

TABLE OF CONTENTS

PART ONE:

How God Revealed "The One" and Hearing God's Voice

Introduction

Do you believe that God told you who your husband would be? Or do you at least wish He would? Does this idea of "The One" spark up a firework show of questions in your head, such as:

- Does "The One" really exist?
- Can God reveal "The One" before we even meet?
- What if I'm wrong in choosing "The One"?
- What if I miss out on "The One"?
- Does everyone have *one*?
- Is it wrong to desire "The One"?

If you can relate to any of these questions, I want to assure you, you are not reading this book by coincidence. This book will provide answers to these questions and help navigate you in hearing God's voice for yourself. You will learn how to discover joy and satisfaction in the midst of your journey. Though this book will be especially helpful to you if you are single, I address those in all relationship seasons, from singles, to courting, engaged, married, and even widowed, divorced, and beyond.

Let's be honest, if it were up to me, I wouldn't have written this book. There is a controversial stigma surrounding this topic of "The One". Yet, I am so happy that I did. This book has provided so much freedom, insight, and confirmation that I never expected to receive just from writing it. I began writing this book with an open mind and an open heart, not necessarily sure of where it would lead, because I too had many questions of my own, even as a married woman.

I believe that many of us need hard truth and distinct direction in this area. My goal in writing this book, with the help of the Holy Spirit, is to make those blurry lines clear. A lot of us have gone astray, given up, or have even been deceived because we weren't sure where God was leading or how He was working in our situation.

If you have had a confusing or discouraging experience in hearing God's voice in a past or current relationship, this book is here to encourage you. I need you to keep pressing forward and trusting God despite the embarrassment and hurt caused. I know it sounds hard, but further along in this book I will explain why it is important and how it is possible.

If you are still hoping—in the hallway of desire—for that door of promise to open in your life, I am here to encourage you to press on in faith, but also enjoy the journey. There is a reason why God shared what He shared with you. There is a reason why you have the desire that you do. There is a reason and perfect purpose for the place that you are in. Don't lose hope.

If you are someone who has received a promise from God, but has begun doubting whether or not you heard wrong or made a mistake, just know this... things may not look the way you expected, but God is working something on the inside of you to bring His will to pass and complete the work He started in you (Philippians 1:6). At the end of the day, He will be glorified. Just hang in there; the best is yet to come.

My Story

Some of you may know my story and some may not. Being raised by a single mother had great implications on how I viewed life, relationships, and what I desired for myself. I grew up desiring to feel loved by a man—I wanted to bury my feelings of abandonment under every relationship I entered. During elementary and middle school, I felt like the ugly duckling. I was constantly made fun of by my peers for the mole on my face (which I consider to be a beauty mark, by the way) and haunted throughout the years by the "not so nice" song from *Outkast* called "Roses" which goes:

Caroline!
See she's the reason for the word "bxxxx"
I hope she's speeding on the way to the club
Trying to hurry up to get to some
Baller or singer or somebody like that
And try to put on her makeup in the mirror
And crash, crash, crash into a ditch!

Everyone LOVED to sing that part of the song to me, and believe me, it still happens to this day! I spent a few of my pre-teen years growing up in Tulsa, Oklahoma. I didn't fit in at my school because the majority the girls there were

13

Caucasian and preppy. The guys never passed me a glimpse. I wasn't ever asked out on a date or to a dance, basically— none one was checking for me.

Plus my style was off and didn't reflect the trends at the time. My mom and aunt bought all my clothes, so it was turtlenecks and corduroys all day, since Oklahoma gets cold. My hair was always pulled back in a boring ponytail and I wore no makeup, because I didn't know how to apply it.

Then, when I moved back to Florida in the eighth grade, something changed. I attended an urban middle where the students were predominantly black and Hispanic. The first day, I was recognized as "the new girl" and word quickly spread around school. For the first time in my life, I was getting the attention I had deeply craved. I recognized that many of the guys seemed interested in me and the girls tried befriending me. What seemed like it would turn into a great year, soon turned into a nightmare.

Truth or dare was the game we played at the time, so I kissed in class, on the school bus to field trips, and so on. I wanted to be cool, so I didn't turn down a dare. I started copying the popular girls and wore fake weaves and false nails because I thought those things would make me beautiful. Eventually I started wearing lip-gloss and putting on eyeliner, and when Christmas break came, I used the money I'd gotten to buy name-brand sneakers, tight shorts, and Apple Bottom jeans. I copied the style trends that were "in" at school and, after returning from Christmas break, everyone noticed my transformation.

At the time, I had developed a body, so when I say that my pants showed everything—they really did. Boys tried talking to me and I got into the habit of having a new boyfriend every week. The "popular girls" that I befriended in the beginning became my worst enemies. They grew to hate me because talked to all the boys they liked. I was threatened constantly. One time I even got a phone call from a girl saying she was going to find me in an alley and cut up my face. I also dealt with cyber bullying on a social network called "Myspace" at the time. Gratefully, God protected me and none of those girls followed through with any physical actions.

My mom was so disappointed in me that year but she also wanted the best for me. The next year she sent me to a charter high school forty-five minutes away from where we lived. My new school was strict about their uniform policy and the student body was a little more diverse. At that point, it didn't even matter. I was so traumatized from the year before; I was committed to keeping a low profile, even though some of the kids said they had heard about me when I got there.

I was tired of my "a boyfriend this week" and "a boyfriend that week" mentality. I wanted something "real" (I still didn't know what real was). I felt the need to fall in love, to one day have a husband of my own, kids, and just be happy. I felt a deep desire to nurture and I wanted to be a wife, for life. I was tired of the vicious cycle of going in and out of different relationships. It all eventually seemed so immature and overrated. I wanted to grow up as soon as possible (which was still pretty immature of me).

As some of you may recall, in my first book, *Before Saying Yes to the Ring*, I talk about how I met Chico and how I had believed he was the one, but it was all just bait from the enemy who was trying to lead me down the wrong path.

He was the first person that I ever thought was supposed to be my husband. I thought God ordained our relationship, but I was so wrong! The proof was not in the pudding and the relationship was completely motivated by my own lust and manipulating tactics.

Then, my second long term relationship was even more convincing. I really thought I had gotten it right. I believed: This is the one God has for me because this man is actually a Christian and we look great on paper! At that time, I called myself a "Christian" and I had gotten saved. But even though that relationship looked godly on the outside, we were compromising and not honoring God with our actions behind closed doors. Though it looked good on paper, it was detestable in God's eyes because I worshipped my relationship and my boyfriend. Those were my gods. This relationship lasted to the point of engagement, but God protected me and cut that off real quick.

The day after breaking off the engagement; I left for college in Tallahassee, Florida, which was a nine-hour drive away from my home. I was so depressed and downtrodden from the situation. My fear of rejection was exposed and the wounds grew even deeper. I couldn't believe that my fiancé had cheated on me and I was too blinded to notice for myself. I had been so anxious to get married, so ready to start a life with him. We even had our future kids' names picked out. To see my dream, my idol, crumble before my eyes, was truly devastating.

God is not lying when He says, "You shall have no other Gods before me" (Exodus 20:3). He is so jealous for you and for me. He desires to be first and foremost in our lives, but because of our hurt, because of our voids, because of our own fleshly desires, we put other things before Him. This should not be—but this was definitely my situation. I didn't want God; I wanted what He could give me. I had a list detailing the perfect husband I wanted and my list was my god. I treated God like my servant.

When I met my actual husband during my freshman year in college, I was backsliding. I went back to my old ways of juggling different guys at a time for mere entertainment to cover up the hurt from my recent breakup. I moved away from God and started partying, clubbing, and dressing provocatively to get the attention of all the college boys.

At the time, my husband wasn't saved and he and his friends owned a daiquiri business with which they co-hosted many college events to sell their drinks. I met him at a spoken word event that they co-hosted one night. I went up to their drink stand and in a flirtatious voice, asked for a free strawberry daiquiri, which he handed to me happily. After the event was over, he came up to me and asked for my number, which I gave him.

For a long time I was ashamed because when we first got married, people would ask us how we met. I was embarrassed because we weren't in the right place spiritually when we first met, and we didn't do everything right. We did not have the perfect Christian love story. Now, I refuse to be ashamed, because God has brought us so far and I want Him to get the glory out of our testimony.

One night after I met my husband, we were already hanging out. By the third night, he was already at my apartment, lying on my bed and, of course, I had on my tight cotton booty shorts. We were listening to music and getting to know each other and he couldn't believe it when I told him I was eighteen, a Christian, was recently engaged, and a virgin waiting until marriage to have sex.

First of all, I wouldn't have believed me either because my words were not matching my actions. I looked older because I had a short pixie haircut at the time that made me seem mature, but I was not mature at all. I surely wasn't acting like a Christian. Him lying next to me in bed, with me in booty shorts on the third day of knowing him didn't really make me seem like I was a virgin waiting till marriage to have sex. It seemed like I was someone he couldn't take seriously.

We continued the casual relationship and eventually he began to sleep over and we were playing house, which was not the plan God had for me. He wanted the real, pure thing for me, not the pretend. God interrupted my tainted relationship by bringing me across Heather Lindsey's blog, which totally changed my perspective on purity and, for the first time in my life, I had an example of what a real godly marriage and relationship looked like. Up to that point, I had no idea of what courtship meant and I was still in the dating mindset. Finally, after much conviction, struggle, and fighting off temptation, I called it quits because the Lord was leading me to separate from Chris.

During the seven months that we were separated, God worked on my husband and me individually. He literally transformed our lives, removed all the trash in our hearts, shattered all our idols, healed us from past hurts, and led us back to having a relationship with Himself. My husband did a total one-eighty. Can you believe he got saved, baptized, started speaking in tongues, reading the bible, started getting revelation from the word, and everything? In that short amount of time, God did such a mighty change and only He can get the credit for it.

Towards the end of those seven months, God revealed to me that Chris would be my future husband. I was so in love with the Lord and dedicated to Him at that point, I didn't even want to hear about no husband. I was so over it. I was finally over the marriage idol, and I had really grown content in my singleness. I even made a three-year vow of singleness to the Lord and said I wouldn't date until after graduation because I wanted to show I could be committed to Him and Him alone. Those months I spent alone with God were honestly some of the best, though hardest, months of my entire life. I had spent my whole life running in and out of relationships and I had never really taken the time to fall in love with Jesus and sit at His feet.

It was so fun and my relationship with Him was more real than any other relationship I had with any human being. Again, I was inspired by Heather Lindsey who shared the idea of having dates with Jesus, movie nights, cooking for Jesus, asking Him what to wear, and so on. God literally became my Love, my Best Friend, my Sustainer, my Everything in that season. The marriage question was far from my mind. I knew it was a desire of mine, and I knew God would fulfill that desire one day, but I didn't expect it to be so soon. I thought it would be years down the line...but God had different plans. For some reason, He wanted Chris and me to be together. Now I know, He wanted us to be married so we could share our testimony and be an example of a godly marriage at such a young age.

Since we've gotten married and started sharing our testimony, we've heard of so many other young couples, some still in college, who pursued purity in their relationship and ended up getting married. People have been inspired by our decision to change our path and do things the right way and I can only thank God for the change He is doing in our generation and all of the new relationships being founded on purity and holiness.

I don't really like to share "how" God revealed who my husband was anymore because I don't think it matters, but I also write about it in *Before Saying "Yes" to the Ring*. What I will share here is how my experience was afterward. At first, it was so hard to accept. I didn't want to believe it because I'd been through it in the past. I thought God told me who my husband was twice before and was wrong both times, so I didn't want to believe it this time and be let down.

Plus, like I mentioned before, I had gotten over Chris and given all my past relationships to God, I was content and not checking for a husband. *Why God? Why would you reveal this to me now, at the start of my three-year vow?* Those ideas are along the lines of my exact thoughts.

I decided if it really were God, there would be nothing I could possibly do to change it or stop it from happening. I wasn't going to manipulate the situation as I had in the past. I wasn't going to try and drop hints and push myself on Chris. If everything worked out, without my interference and without it becoming a distraction in my life, then that was the only way I would know it was God's will.

Everything came together so smoothly. It was summertime when God revealed Chris was going to be my husband, right before my sophomore semester in school, but before that, God told me I would see Chris again when I went to Tallahassee. Initially I rejected this thought because I believed it was merely a distraction from the enemy, but it was actually God preparing me for what was to come. Because I didn't know at the time Chris would be my husband one day, it didn't make sense why I would see him again, especially in the midst of the three-year commitment I had made to God. But weeks down the road, when God revealed that Chris was going to be my husband, I started having peace and believing I would see him again. I still had my guard up, just in case it was the enemy, and was unwilling to expect anything to happen.

I decided in my heart that I was going to let Chris pursue me. By then, I had listened to so many sermons concerning God's purpose for creating man and woman, and how the woman was created to be a helpmeet to the man. Marriage is about purpose, so if I'm supposed to be someone's helpmeet, that person should actually need "help" with something. That person should be busy about God's business and not just sitting around distracted by the things of the world and doing nothing.

When I reconnected with Chris, as the Holy Spirit led, the helpmeet portion of the puzzle was confirmed. Chris started sharing with me all of the visions and plans God had given him in order for him to help and contribute to the body of Christ. Even though he hadn't taken full action on those plans yet and was simply laying down the bare bone foundation, I was able to see how God could use my talents and abilities to help Chris and build upon that vision for the future.

Now you're probably wondering, so how exactly did you reconnect with Chris? Well here's how I got to the point of meeting Chris again... and I say, "meeting" him again, because he was such a different person the second time around, we both were. It was as if I was meeting a new him for the first time and the old him was gone.

"You were taught, with regard to your former way of life, to put off your old self, which is being corrupted by its deceitful desires; to be made new in the attitude of your minds; and the put on the new self, created to be like God in true righteousness and holiness." - Ephesians 4:22-24

Before the end of the summer, my plans to return to school were set in place. For the fall semester, I was supposed to be moving into a scholarship house—a community home for girls with good academics who pay almost nothing to live there. Chris lived in a Christian community home, which he moved to during his season of transformation. He chose to get out of his old environment and distance himself from old friends and roommates in order to focus on growing his relationship with God while resisting all forms of temptation. He took extreme measures because he was serious about his walk with God. Chris heard about this home through his cousin, who is also my friend. She was the same cousin I teamed up with to buy Chris his first bible before he and I split up and we both remained connected even after Chris and I stopped talking. She was also my ride back to school in Tallahassee.

So, as the day approached to ride back to school, the Holy Spirit whispered to me and said, "You're going to see Chris again." I thought, *Lord, if this is you, I'm sure it will happen. I don't know how you plan on doing it, but we'll see.*

Remember, even though I knew he was going to be my husband, in my mind I wouldn't be connecting with him until at least three years down the road because of my vow of singleness. In my mind, it didn't make sense for us to reconnect at the time we did. I didn't understand what God was trying to do and I couldn't see myself holding on to the secret of what I knew for three entire years while being in Chris' presence and just being his friend. If that was the case, I would have rather stayed single and focused on God. I did not want to have to worry about that becoming a distraction, growing impatient, and fighting back and forth about whether or not what God said was true…only to find out at the end of the three years, Chris marries someone else.

That's why I was so skeptical during the whole process, while still leaving some room for a little hope and expectation. I left room for God to lead the situation until I was in complete peace about it. I wanted to be sure that I was really hearing from God and not just hoping I was hearing from God in order to satisfy my own emotions.

I needed to see that Chris was in agreement with what I thought God was telling me. That was one of the first things I looked for when we reconnected, and it's exactly what I got from him. Even though we had gone our separate ways and had changed, Chris wanted to be with me just as much as I wanted to be with him and he knew it was the Lord's will—he knew we would get married one day. It was not a one-sided thing. He wasn't being forced upon me and neither was I being pushed upon him. It all just happened *naturally*.

It is okay to want to be attracted to your mate. God cares about you, even the little details of your life; He doesn't skip over. You want to know my opinion of Chris? *That brother is fine!* I was like, "Okay, God; you really did have the best in store…you made him just how I like him!" Of course, overtime you can grow in physical attraction towards your spouse; I do believe beauty is in the eye of the beholder. In that case, they will have other things about them that encourage that physical attraction between you both. For example, they should also be kind, gentle, and have many other positive qualities to them. Looks aren't everything and can surely fade away any minute. If that person has a nasty attitude, no direction, nothing to contribute and you find yourself being pressured into marrying them because you think God told you to, but you have absolutely no peace about it, be very careful!

God will never pressure you to do anything. He will prompt you, He will lead you, but He will never pressure you to the point where it's stressing you out and feels like an overwhelming burden. That's the enemy. Jesus came to take the pressure off. He says,

"Come to me, all you who are weary and burdened, and I will give you rest. Take my yoke upon you and learn from me, for I am gentle and humble in heart, and you will find rest for your souls. For my yoke is easy and my burden is light." – Matthew 11:30

So on the day that Chris' cousin and I were to travel to Tallahassee, we had planned on leaving in the morning to get a head start on the nine-hour drive. From the beginning, it seemed as if everything was keeping us from going along with our plan. She had some issues she had to deal with concerning her family and on top of that, she also had different errands to run for her mother before we left. From time to time she would text me to update me on what was going on; all the while the time was getting pushed back. Also, it was storming heavily that day (we were in the middle of hurricane season in Florida), and so we had to drive even slower on the roads. This was clearly all a part of God's plan.

When we finally got on the road, I calculated the time it would take for me to arrive at my scholarship house. I realized I would be late, and I wondered if I'd still be able to check in. When moving in, it is mandatory to go through the process of inspecting your room, filling out some paperwork, and then getting your keys. I knew we would be reaching Tallahassee no earlier than midnight so I tried to contact my house manager to see if she would still be able to check me in. I could not reach her and when I contacted my roommate, she said she wouldn't be there to open the door for me.

When I communicated this to Chris' cousin, she thought it would be safest if I just went straight home with her, spent the night in her room, and then she would take me to the scholarship house to check in the next morning. I couldn't believe all this was happening. I was thinking, *No. I am NOT going to see Chris* and tried to fight the inevitable with my thoughts. What God had spoken to me seemed to get more real and real by the minute, and I was quite nervous about the whole situation. They both lived in the same Christian community home and though I didn't want to expect anything from the brief visit… deep down inside, I could see God's plan unravel before my eyes. It was such a surreal experience.

We arrived extremely late and everyone was sound asleep in the house. I got my things together, went straight to the bed she had prepared for me in her room, and went to sleep. When I woke up the next morning, I went to the bathroom to get ready for her to take me home. I walked out of the bathroom, turned to go back to her room and prepare my things, and then I saw Chris. He was so shocked because he didn't expect to see me. His eyes were wide and he went on to say:

"Kar!" (Pronounced 'care') with great surprise. "What are you doing here?" he asked.
"It's a looooong story," I said.

After I deposited my bathroom stuff back in the room, Chris asked me to join him in the living room to do some catching up. That moment of catching up brought so much confirmation to the entire situation. I finally accepted in my heart that it had been the Holy Spirit all long telling me I would see Chris when I went back to Tallahassee. It was the Holy Spirit who had revealed ahead of time that Chris was going to be my husband.

We sat and I listened as he shared his new life and journey that he had been on. He was so excited about Jesus, the bible, and told me about different revelations he had received and written down in his notebook. He told me he was celibate and had made the decision to remain pure until marrying his future wife. He also shared his struggles and feats in dealing with temptation. Different women from his past had tried reaching out to him but by the grace of God, he resisted the temptation and pressed further into God's presence. He was a completely different person! He talked differently, thought differently, and even walked differently. I was shocked and blown away at what God had done in just seven months!

I was thinking: *that thing you just said about waiting for your wife is just so sexy. You have no idea that I'm going to be her. Yes, Lord!* He shared a vision with me that he'd had about a little girl sitting down reading the bible, though he didn't know what it meant. It resonated with me because, during our time apart, God had given me dreams of a giggly and curly haired baby girl who was going to be my daughter. Can you believe I am writing this book as a six-month pregnant woman? And by the time you read this book, I'll either be close to my due date or have already given birth…isn't God so faithful? It took three years for me to see that promise come to pass, but regardless, God has been faithful in keeping His promises.

We knew the name of our baby girl even before we got married because God shared it with me on a bus ride to one of my classes. I will never forget just sitting there, minding my own business on the way to my next class and I heard the Holy Spirit whisper "Evelyn".

Evelyn? Who is Evelyn? I thought.
"The name of your future daughter," He said.

Later on, I looked up the name Evelyn and it's a Hebrew name meaning "life". Eventually when I told Chris this, he was in agreement with the name and we decided Michelle would be her middle name, which means "Gift from God" in

Hebrew. So, Evelyn Michelle is a "Gift of life from God" to us.

Honestly, that promise for a child held me over during my first year and a half of marriage because we had been trying to conceive for months before we actually got pregnant and I was really getting discouraged and started to question my dreams, wondering if there was something wrong with me. Then I realized, it just wasn't God's timing for us to have children that early in our marriage. By the time Evelyn is here, we will have two full years of marriage out of the way, and Chris and I needed those two years to grow as a couple and individually, in the roles God prepared for us. Especially since we got married quicker than normal after meeting each other, I believe God wanted to give us that time to grow together.

So, while we were sitting in the living room catching up, and I was getting all this confirmation, I heard the Holy Spirit say, "Chris is going to help you move in today." I was fighting my thoughts. I could not believe that I was sitting there with Chris at that very moment and all of the confirmation that was going forth felt like a dream, it was too good to be true. I thought, *Nah, Alicia's taking me home.* Just then, she runs out all frazzled and says, "I'm running late for the wedding, would you mind if Chris took you home? And Chris would you mind taking Karolyne home?" Come to find out she had a wedding that day and was apart of it.

He said he didn't mind. So we went outside while she was getting ready, and he started moving all of my boxes and bags out of her car and into his. When we left to go to my scholarship house, she was still getting ready for the wedding. I feel like the reason the Holy Spirit told me everything that would happen ahead of time, is so I would be encouraged to know that I actually do hear his voice, especially after getting so much confirmation. Everything was coming to pass just as He said.

Chris helped me move in and took all of my bags and things out of the car. I met my roommate, house manager, did the inspection, and got the keys, as well as a rundown of the house rules. I realize now that I moved into that house and out of my apartment during the perfect season. Now that I look back, I can see that it was God setting me up for success in my courtship and engagement.

The house had many rules and standards; we had visitation hours and they were very strict on guys visiting the house. Eventually, when we got together, Chris and I usually hung out during the day if he was off work, sometimes in the evening, but there were always people around so we had the accountability we needed in pursuing purity. At the

Christian home where he stayed with many other believers, there too were rules and they were even stricter and specifically geared towards fostering spiritual growth. Our new environments were beneficial in keeping us on track to where God was leading us. When we had our own apartments and we were playing house, God wasn't pleased.

So after Chris helped me moved in, we chatted for a little while more and, based on the circumstances, we realized that our seven-month period apart had practically been broken out of our control. We went on to just being friends for some time and eventually we began hanging out.

Apparently, Chris had gotten several visions about me being his wife and just had a deep feeling that I was. A few weeks into us hanging out, he started this game that went something like this:

Chris: "I know."

Me: "You know what?"

Chris: "I know what you don't know."

Me: "No, I know what you think you know that I don't know."

Then one day we went out to eat and we got into the "I know" game. I was just hoping the game would last for the next two and a half years and we would leave it at that because I was still on my three-year vow of singleness to God and I was not looking to break it. Then Chris said,

"Do you really know?"
I said, "Yes, I know."
"How do you know? Did you see a wedding dress?"

I gave him this piercing look and thought, *"What the heck, bro? You just messed up the game!"* then I turned my head to the side, and I looked down and sighed. I began by saying, "This is awkward, awkward, AWKWARD." It was blank, quiet, for a good minute. Then I told him the story about how I knew, and he began to share his visions with me as well.

We got into a conversation about how crazy it was that we knew, but also how cool it was. We were talking about purpose. There must have been a reason God would reveal it to us both at that time. We discussed how we must have a special assignment and a duty to stay focused. We didn't think we'd be getting married anytime soon because Chris acknowledged my vow and purity ring and he respected it.

As we continued just being friends, people began to ask questions like, "Is he your boyfriend?" and "Are you guys talking?" Many people would even make comments like, "He looks like the hubby type" or "I can see y'all getting married" and I'd say, "Well, I don't know. We'll see about that." It was a huge secret. The only people who knew were God, Chris, and I, along with his cousin and my best friend, who I eventually told. I felt the peace to tell her towards the end of the summer.

Soon enough I became torn. I became torn with the fact that I was so determined to do this three-year singleness thing and Chris, my future husband, was right there in my face. Not only that, for as much as I hung around him and still claimed I was single and nothing was going on, our relationship began looking ungodly to everyone, and it began to seem as if I was hiding something bad, even though I wasn't.

"Abstain from all appearance of evil." -1 Thessalonians 5:22

My best friend eventually brought this issue to my attention...

"You and Chris might as well court. It looks to everyone like that's what you guys are doing anyway."
"But Bestie! I made a three-year vow to God that I wouldn't."

"That's honorable," she said. "But YOU made the three-year vow. God did not tell you to, and it just may not be His will for you to be single for three years. You have to pray and go to Him about that. I am sure that He sees your heart and loves that you would even commit to making a vow like that to Him, but regardless, He just may have other plans for you, so just make sure it's His will that you continue doing this three-year thing."

One of the biggest mistakes I made was announcing my three-year vow to the world. Now that the vow was in question, my reliability and the validity of my words were in question, too. That goes to say, don't share vows you have made with the whole world unless you have completed them. Special commitments like that should be kept secret anyway.

Finally, I went to God about it. I had been ignoring Him and fighting Him on this thing the whole time. I did not want to hear what He had to say because I knew what it was. I mean, it was obvious; He brought Chris back into my life for a reason.

God revealed who my husband was so I could prepare and equip myself to be with the man I was specifically designed for. God revealed who Chris was so I could pray for him by name, and prepare to cater to his needs and growth so we could get to the place where we were both ready to be married.

After praying, I realized it was true. God was moving me in a direction opposite of my three-year vow and I finally accepted it. I had a conversation with Chris to let him know that I was honored by him being willing to wait for me, but I felt like it was okay if we moved forward, if he wanted to do so.

Can you see the triangle? I wanted to show God my willingness to honor Him and in return, God showed me that Chris was willing to honor me. Chris and I talked about it and decided to be boyfriend and girlfriend. About a month later, we were engaged, and within nine months we were married.

The process I had prolonged—spending years running away from God and jumping from relationship to relationship—the process I tried to speed up and manipulate many times myself, happened in a matter of months because I finally decided to let go, be content, find my satisfaction in the Lord and trust Him with my life. Whew, you would be surprised at what God can do in your life when you honestly let go and trust Him. Keep in mind that every story is different, so I'm not telling you that you will be married nine-months from now! But I am telling you that your love story and life story will always be better when you sit back and let God write it for you.

Everyone's Story is Different

Not any one person is the same and the relationship each and every one of us have with God is unique. God knows us perfectly, more than we even know ourselves, and He communicates things to us in a way that we will understand if we listen. What if God inspires someone of his or her purpose through a movie? Maybe that person is very visual, and it helps when they can see things play out before them. Or what if God reveals someone else's purpose to them with the help and guidance of someone who they truly respect and look up to, knowing that they would be very attentive to that person's leadership. God will even speak to you directly, if you're willing to listen. He may even try to show something in a way you do not understand, because He wants you to take the time to seek Him, pray, and wait on Him long enough to listen. Whichever way God chooses to do it, trust that it's in your best interest.

We often try to compare our lives and our stories to those around us. The enemy convinces us to do this because He wants us to feel inadequate, to think God has forgotten about us or to think He has put more effort into someone else's life and journey apart from our own. This is what bible says:

"There will be trouble and distress for every human being who does evil: first the Jew, then for the Gentile; but glory, honor and peace for everyone who does good: first for the Jew, then for the Gentile. For God does not show favoritism." – Romans 2: 9-11

Jew or Gentile, Annie or Susie, Grace or Mary, God shows no favoritism. He created us all, and He wishes the best for us all. We will all have to reap what we sow, whether good or bad.

"The Lord is not slow in keeping His promise, as some understand slowness. Instead, He is patient with you, not wanting anyone to perish, but everyone to come to repentance." - 2 Peter 3:9

The thing holding us back from truly receiving all that God has for us is not our skin color, not our education level, not our status in the church, but our sin. God abhors sin and He cannot bless us if we are still living under the curse. Look at the example in James 3:10-12 which says:

"Out of the same mouth come praise and cursing. My brothers and sisters, this should not be. Can both fresh water

and salt water flow from the same spring? My brothers and
sisters, can a fig tree bear olives, or a grapevine bear figs?
Neither can a salt spring produce fresh water."

You put yourself in a bad position when you live a life of
sin, and you put yourself in a favorable position when you
choose to live a life of righteousness in Christ. That doesn't
mean your life will be perfect when you live righteously. But
you are in a favorable position because you know how to
access the tools you need... the grace, the armor, the hand of
God on your side to help you every step of the way. You
aren't as vulnerable to failure, defeat, and dismay. Sin makes
us vulnerable; an open-target for the enemy to cause
destruction in our lives.

Because of what Jesus did on the cross, and because of
who we are in Him when we accept Him, we become set
apart. Apart from Jesus, we are all the same... just evil
sinners. Through Christ, we are no longer sinners; we put on
the new man, created to be like God in true righteousness
and holiness (Ephesians 4:24). That is the only thing that will
cause anyone to live a favored life, and in that case, God is
not favoring the person, but favoring whom that person is in
Christ. It's not about God favoring Billy over you; it's about
God favoring Billy's new man over his old man. It's about

God favoring you in Jesus over you in the world. When we truly live for God, we don't have to worry, we don't have to beg Him to fulfill His promises and purpose in our life, it is already done. Take some time to meditate these scriptures and rest in these promises of God's favor:

"The eyes of the LORD are on the righteous, and His ears are attentive to their cry; but the face of the LORD is against those who do evil, to blot out their name from the earth."
- Psalm 24:15-16

"The righteous person may have many troubles, but the LORD delivers him from them all; He protects all his bones, not one of them will be broken." - Psalm 34:19-20

"I was young and now I am old, yet I have never seen the righteous forsaken or their children begging bread."
- Psalm 37:25

"Surely, LORD, you bless the righteous; you surround them with your favor as with a shield." - Psalm 5:12

But Lord, I have been good, I am righteous, I serve at church, I'm over three ministries, I have been celibate for years! When is my time, God? Everyone around me is getting married, having babies... some of them don't even serve you, but it seems as if you have blessed them, favored them, and forgotten about me! ...Does this sound like you? Or have you been there? You see, I have, and I have learned that things always look better than they seem when we are looking at everybody else and looking at ourselves, rather than looking to God. We see the glamorized highlight reels through social media. We see the perfect relationship, perfect little cute babies with the perfect hair, beautiful women with the perfect body, clothes, and the perfect makeup and we feel like we're missing out.

Here's what we don't see... we don't see when the couple we idolize when they're fighting and are at each other's throats behind closed doors. We don't see the missing father in that cute little baby's life. We don't see the throw up that the beautiful women just flushed down the toilet because she is insecure about her own body and looks. We don't see all the scars under all the beautifully and perfectly contoured makeup. We see all that is temporary, and fail to recognize eternity. Or, we focus on ourselves and only see me, me, and me. We pity ourselves and expect God to join in on our pity party, knowing good and well we should just trust Him, but we're so afraid. We're so afraid that if we trust Him, we'll be let down. We're afraid that if we really let go of that thing and give it to Him, He will forget. What is up with us always thinking God is going to forget? Remember, the bible says, "Indeed, the very hairs of your head are all numbered" (Luke 12:7). Don't be afraid; you are worth more to God than the sparrows, and He even takes care of them. What makes you think that this God, the Creator of all things, would skip over even the most miniscule details of your life?

When we take our eyes off of everyone else and off of ourselves, and put them on God, we will finally be able to know and see who we truly are in Him. His word is our mirror and we were made in His image. Don't be like the man who they talk about in James 1: 23-24, and it says, "Anyone who listens to the word but does not do what it says is like someone who looks at his face in a mirror and, after looking at himself, goes away and immediately forgets what he looks like." Sister, you can't say you trust God and keep comparing your portion to everyone else's. You can't call yourself righteous and say you serve here and there when you don't even remember who you are or what you look like.

Look at God and He will remind you. Keep your eyes on Christ. The bible says, "Delight yourself in the LORD and He will give you the desires of your heart." – Psalm 37:4. Meaning, when you truly keep your eyes on Jesus, and get them off yourself and everyone else, your desires change and they become His desires. When you share the same desires as God shares for you, you won't miss out on anything. The bible also says,

"Seek ye first the kingdom of God, and His righteousness; and all these things shall be added unto you" - Matthew 6:33

So what are you seeking? Are you truly seeking God? Or are you seeking a husband? Are you seeking the perfect fairytale love story or coveting your sister's life? Copying her and wishing you could be just like her? There is only one thing we should be seeking and that's God's kingdom and His righteousness. Remember, righteousness sets us apart, and after we have that, everything else will fall into place.

How to Hear God's Voice

When you have a personal relationship with God, you should be able to distinguish the voice of God as opposed to the voice of the devil or your own voice. Just like any relationship, when you have a best friend, or when you have a husband and you spend so much time talking to them and you communicate with them on a daily basis, you will know their voice. You can be in a crowded arena with that person and they'll call out to you and you'll look up because you recognize their voice. It's the same thing with God. There could be a lot of things going on in our life, and spiritually, we may be in a crowded room but we'll still hear the gentle voice of the Holy Spirit speaking to us and we'll know it's Him if we're actually spending time in His word.

Nowadays, many of us are lazy and we don't really want to spend time with God to the point where we are really in tune with the Holy Spirit. We just want to immediately hear God's audible voice thunder down from heaven and say something like "THIS IS YOUR HUSBAND" or "THIS IS THE MAN I WANT YOU TO MARRY!" This is selfish of us; God wants us to seek Him. His word says, "You will seek me and find me, when you seek me with all your heart" (Jeremiah 29:13). So maybe if you're not sure whether or not you're hearing God in your life, it's not because God does not want to have a relationship with you and it's not because He doesn't care to reveal things about your future, but maybe God is saying, "I want you to seek me more." Maybe He's saying, "No, I'm not going to speak to you in an audible voice. No, I'm not going to give you a prophetic dream. No, I'm not going to give you all these signs and wonders because I want you to believe in ME."

"Then Jesus told Him, "Because you have seen me, you have believed; blessed are those who have not seen and yet have believed." -John 20:29

That's why I say it doesn't matter how God revealed to me that Chris was going to be my husband. If you're depending on the way God revealed it to me, and hoping he'll reveal it to you the same way, then you've missed it.

If you want the Lord to reveal things about your life, secret things, you need to keep your eyes on Him—not on anyone else and their story. If you want to get on God's holy mountain, you need to be focused on Him and getting closer to Him in order to climb it. If you look anywhere else, you will fall down on the way up.

People say, "Well, God doesn't speak to me, He just doesn't!" God is always speaking. He is an eternal God and the bible describes even His word as eternal. Matthew 24:35

says, "Heaven and Earth will pass away but my words will never pass away." His words will never pass away because His word is eternal. Meaning, God is speaking now, He's been speaking, and He's going to be speaking tomorrow—God is always speaking. But are you listening? Are you reading His word? Are you available to listen to the truth He sends forth? Or do you have itchy ears and pick and choose from His word and from all these different sources, all these different people on social media, whatever it is your *flesh* wants to hear?

Another reason why we may not feel like God is speaking at some points in our lives is because we may be going through a test. As the saying goes, "The teacher doesn't speak during the test." You may have had this season where you got saved and you felt like you were so close to God. You were just so excited and on fire for God, always in your word, always getting new revelations about life and your eyes were opened up and God taught you so many things.

So, what are you doing with all those things God taught you in the last season? Did you just forget about it? You are in the test right now and God is not going to baby you anymore. Maybe He taught you about patience, about waiting on Him and seeking Him. Maybe He taught you about contentment, about keeping your eyes on Christ and off of this world.

Maybe He taught you about having faith, about enduring, about persevering. He wants you to apply all those things in THIS season.

When God is speaking, it's either directly from His word or in line with His word. You will have peace about it. When the enemy is speaking, it's contrary to God's word or it's a twisted version of God's word. If you don't know God's word, how will you be able to decipher whether or not what you're hearing is a twisted version of it? That takes true attention to detail and a true knowledge and holistic understanding of God and scripture. The enemy will cut and paste scripture and leave parts of the bible out. You need to know God's word in a holistic sense, not just a few popular bible verses. Knowing the God of the word and having a personal relationship with Him, is also crucial.

Furthermore, when it comes to what you think, it doesn't even matter if it's you because you can be in the flesh today and in the spirit tomorrow. So if you're in the flesh today, you'll be in accordance with what the enemy is saying, and if you're in the spirit tomorrow, you'll be in accordance with what God is saying. So it's not as complicated as, "Is it me, God, or the devil?" It's as simple as, "Is this contrary to God's word?" and "Do I have peace about this?" You should be concerned with what God is saying. Who cares what you're saying? Or why care what the devil is saying? What is God saying? When you find that out, when you find that His word lines up, pray and go forth with the leading of the Holy Spirit.

If God told you something, and you're looking for confirmation... the confirmation that God said it, is when it happens. Now, if you manipulate the situation during the process and you get into a marriage with that person, you will always have those daunting questions in the back of your mind: *Was it really God?* Or *Did we get married because I manipulated the situation?* That person will start showing their true colors and the next thing you know, you'll start entertaining thoughts of divorce because you're not even sure if you ended up with the right person.

If God told you something, don't try calling that person; don't try stalking that person on social media. If God is telling you, "Be still my Daughter", just be still and know that He is God (Psalm 46:10). Then when you are finally pursued and you didn't say anything, and God is getting glory out of your relationship, you'll know that it was Him.

So are you ready to put your relationship with God first and are you ready to put God first in your relationship? Or are you just asking God, "Reveal my husband, reveal to my husband!" If that's the case, Sis, you're not worried about God. You want Him to reveal who your husband will be because that is where your heart is. That is your true desire. We need to get back to the point where we desire God more than we desire anything else.

We need so stay focused. Have you even asked God if it is His will for you to be married? Marriage is not for everybody. Or do you just feel pressured because everyone else seems to desire marriage? Or because your aunts and everybody keeps asking you when you're going to have a boyfriend? When you're going to have kids? You're sitting around waiting for marriage, waiting for your next breakthrough, waiting for this and that, when the only thing we should be waiting on is the Lord and His return. So who and what are you waiting on? Today could be your last day. Jesus could come tomorrow. You don't know when you'll take your last breath on this earth. So if you're waiting for anything and that thing is not God, you are distracted.

I'm not telling you that you're shallow if you have a desire to be in a relationship, because we all need relationships. But the foundation of any relationship, and to make it truly work and to see the fruit of the relationship, comes from having a relationship with Christ. So, if you are dying to have all these relationships with all these other people and you think it's going to fulfill you, but you truly haven't developed a relationship with Jesus Christ, you've missed it. My marriage is only richer when my relationship with God is growing. When my relationship with God is stagnant, you can tell. My husband and I will constantly argue, I'll be angry, bitter, and all over the place. You have to keep that connection with God and keep Him first in your relationship, in your life, and everything else will follow.

God Told Me

Oh, the dreaded phrase many are annoyed to hear and others are afraid to use, "God told me." People get so antsy around this phrase and of course, I understand why they would. In the past, the phrase "God told me" has been used and abused in many destructive ways and still is to this day. There has been a trend created where people blame God for their actions and use God as an excuse to do what their own flesh desires. A lot of times, many things that people say God told them to do, directly contradict the bible and the very character of God...and God is the same now and forever. So what is it? Is God lying? Did He change His mind? Or is it us?

With that being said, we also can't put God in a box. God can in fact speak to us and tell us things. He spoke to men throughout the whole bible; actually, the Bible itself, was written by men who were inspired by the Holy Spirit. So we can't sit here and grow bitter and act like God wouldn't speak to someone or share something with him or her about his or her future. Who are we to judge that? Of course, you can judge by the fruit, but as long as what they are saying doesn't contradict what God said in His word, God could have very well told them something. You ask, why? Why would God tell them that? And you try to judge the person and conjure reasons in your mind why God wouldn't speak to them on that level. You may think *that person isn't so great of a*

Christian, they can't even do this simple thing right or that simple thing right, God wouldn't talk to them on that level, but how do you know what God would do? What if God is revealing something specific to them so they can actually get their life together? Why do we constantly assume that we know if God would do this, and know if God would do that when the bible clearly says that God works in mysterious ways? (Isaiah 45:15) And when it says, His thoughts are above our thoughts and ways above our ways. (Isaiah 55:8)

If you're the super-holy Christian who is bitter because other people are hearing from God and you're thinking, *but God never shared anything like that with me. God didn't reveal who my future husband was, so why would He reveal it to her?* You have to realize that your spiritual walk and relationship with God is different from the next person. God is not going to deal with you the same way He deals with everyone else.

"Ask me and I will tell you remarkable secrets you do not know about things to come." - Jeremiah 33:3

It is clear in God's word that He does share secrets of the future with His children. Here are two important keywords to keep in mind though, "secrets" and "relationship". Our relationship with God is private. Everything that happens between God and us is not to be broadcasted to the world. That's why the bible says, "But when you pray, go into your room, close the door and pray to your Father, who is unseen. Your Father, who sees what is done in secret, will reward you" (Matthew 6:6). When God tells you something, don't just log on to Facebook the next minute and say, "God just told me to start this business! This is the vision God gave me…" Or go to all the ladies in the women's ministry at your church, some of whom may already be gossiping about you, and say, "Guess what? God told me who my husband was! It's Danny on the prayer team."

Slow down Sis, did you even consult God about that? The devil has ears, and the people who you may be telling things may have demons in them, which have ears, too. If the enemy didn't already hear the news (he is not omniscient, he can only be at one place at a time), you better believe his demons will report the information back to him. Then, before you know it, all these attacks will start coming up against you and you'll begin to question if God really told you that because you opened up your mouth out of season. Then you'll be trying harder than ever to cling closely to that promise that you're not even sure about. Dealing with unnecessary tests and trials that God didn't even intend for you to go through in the first place. You'll get worn out and go around telling everyone, "I must've heard God wrong" or "I guess I missed God" and now you've got people looking at you with the side-eye and God is unable to get the glory out of your situation because you opened the door for the enemy to come and cause confusion in your life.

Remember, the bible says, "For God is not the author of confusion, but of peace, as in all the churches of the saints." (1 Corinthians 14:33) When you open up your mouth and share your business, the enemy will try to confuse you through other people and bring distractions into your life. He'll use the people closest to you, maybe even your family, maybe someone you highly respect and have them say, "Are you sure God said that?" Or they might say, "God wouldn't say that. I don't see why God would say that." Like my Pastor, Cornelius Lindsey always says, "I don't expect people to understand what God told me because He didn't tell them, He told me."

Don't waste your breath trying to convince others of the promise God has given you. It's hard enough for you to believe it yourself. You're trying to present to them all the confirmations you've received from the Lord and you may even be thinking you're crazy and you conjured this up in your mind. Why even put yourself through that? Whatever

God told you; He told it to you in private, during your quiet time for a reason. He could've written it in the sky for everyone to see, but He didn't choose to do that. God wants to protect us.

When we don't fully believe He's protecting us, we fell the need to step in and protect ourselves. In doing that, we cause even more harm to ourselves. We think that sharing what God told us with someone else will make us feel safe. We want to feel like we have someone to talk to. But if we could just trust God, and know He has everything under control, if we could just trust in due season that when He's ready to put us on blast, He will, we would save ourselves much struggle, much heartache, and much embarrassment. The process would be much smoother and more peaceful. God is there for us to talk to. God is there to comfort us. But why do we continually take the sacred opportunities that we have to spend with God, and share them with everyone else? To have a secret between you and God is such a special thing. To know that you and the Creator of the universe are on one accord and in this together is so precious.

Now, I do not say this to say that God will not have you share anything with anyone, ever. Sometimes God will specifically lead you to share what He has revealed with you to someone else or some other people. In that case, as long as

God is leading you, it's fine, but you really need to be discerning to make sure you are not being led by your emotions.

Just because you heard someone is going through a similar situation, does not mean you should share any information with him or her. It's natural for us to want to gravitate towards people we feel we can relate to. As humans, it makes us feel comfortable and safe, especially if we're dying for confirmation. But let God be the judge of who you share information with, even in situations like that, where it just seems so right. When you are led by the Holy Spirit to share information with specific people, those people won't drain you—they will encourage you. They may even play a pivotal part of the whole process and a big role in God's plan for you, you may not even know it, but remain obedient and continue to be led by Him.

Sometimes God will tell people what He told you, and send them directly to you as a confirmation, but do not be deceived. Pray after every encounter you have with someone you think you're receiving confirmation from. It may not be from God. The devil knows how we, as believers, operate. He studies us and he studies how we interact with God and one another so He can try to copy God and deceive us, having us think it's God when it's not Him at all.

You may have been told that a certain person is your husband, and even though they don't live a biblical lifestyle, you, for some reason, are seeking confirmation. Sis, the devil sent a false prophet to tell you that this person was going to be your husband or he placed a false thought in your mind and you thought it was the Holy Spirit. Now that the enemy has lured you in, because you've been telling everyone and their momma you think this may be your husband, and he's heard you say, "But I'm just waiting on a confirmation," he sends you his own confirmation. He sends a false prophet to tell you, "God told me this man is going to be your husband." You're so ecstatic and happy and say, "Thank you, Lord! This is the confirmation I needed!" Still you're not at total peace because the true Holy Spirit is tugging at your heart. He's revealing to you, "This guy goes to the club every weekend, he fornicates, he smokes, he's not of Me." But you're desperate, so even in the midst of the confusion, even though you know you and that man would be unequally yoked, you cling to that false confirmation, you cling to that false hope because you idolize marriage and you're so desperate to be married.

You think it will look good to everyone on the outside and you think of the perfect love story you will have. You can't wait to tell people that *God told you* and you can't wait to tell them about the confirmation you received because it makes you feel special and holy to know that God loves you so much that He would reveal your future husband to you. Even though, on the inside, you know everything is wrong. You think you can change this man. You say, "I know he's not perfect now, but if God told me he's going to be my husband, I am going to stick by his side and make this work."

Sis, you can't change that man! I'm just being honest with you. I've been there and tried that. I had to leave Chris alone so God could change him, and I had to move on because he and I were unequally yoked in that season. Do you see the cycle? Do you see how having idols in your heart makes you easy bait for the enemy? That's why the bible says, "Be alert and of sober mind. Your enemy the devil prowls around like a roaring lion looking for someone to devour" (1 Peter 5:8). The devil goes to the weakling and he attacks our weaknesses. That's why were instructed:

"Guard your heart above all else, for it determines the course of your life." - Proverbs 4:23

Guard your heart from men you know are no good for you. Guard your heart from useless idols. Our safety is in seeking the Lord. Our safety is in trusting the Lord and not taking things into our own hands and jumping into the wrong situation in the wrong season.

"Did God really tell me who my husband was?"

At times, you may question if God really told you who your husband was or if you made it up in your head. From my experience, there are a few things I recognized which led me to know that God surely did tell me that Chris was going to be my husband.

1. **The Holy Spirit encouraged me to work on my relationship, and to not run away from it.**

    When times grew tough during my courtship and engagement season, and when Chris was getting on my last nerve, God encouraged me to grow in many areas. He encouraged me to be patient with Chris, to pay attention to the way I talked to him, to make sure I was being loving and compassionate, and bearing the fruits of the Spirit. With relationships I had before, this was not the case. Instead of the Holy Spirit encouraging me to work on my relationship, I was constantly convicted of my sin within the relationship, either feeling trapped in the relationship, or a push to leave that man alone! Chris was the first guy I was ever with where it seemed like God was in agreement and leading me through our courtship and engagement.

"So I say, walk by the Spirit, and you will not gratify the desires of the flesh. For the flesh desires what is contrary to the Spirit, and the Spirit what is contrary to the flesh. They are in conflict with each other, so that you are not to do whatever you want. But if you are led by the Spirit, you are not under the law. The acts of the flesh are obvious: sexual immorality, impurity and debauchery; idolatry and witchcraft; hatred, discord, jealousy, fits of rage, selfish ambition, dissensions, factions and envy; drunkenness, orgies, and the like. I warn you, as I did before, that those who live like this will not inherit the kingdom of God. But the fruit of the Spirit is love, joy, peace, forbearance, kindness, goodness, faithfulness, gentleness and self-control. Against such things there is no law." – Galatians 5:16-23

2. **Our relationship drew me closer to God, not away from Him.**

Because God was so involved in our relationship, and He was the center of it, we were able to keep our eyes on Him. The other relationships that I had been in were different. Instead of having my eyes on God, I created many

68

idols in my heart. In the past, I would idolize my spouse; I would meditate on thoughts of the future, sex, and things that were ultimately self-seeking and feeding my flesh. When I was with Chris, we ran away from those traps and we ran closer to God. We grew spiritually, both individually and together.

"When tempted, no one should say, "God is tempting me." For God cannot be tempted by evil, not does he tempt anyone; but each person is tempted when they are dragged away by their own evil desire and enticed." – James 1: 13-14

3. There was good fruit on his tree.

Only time will tell if the fruit on someone's tree reflects the true nature of who they claim to be. Before I could be convinced that what God told me was true, I had to see some progression in Chris' walk with Christ. It had to be real; it had to be all God. I wanted to be sure that he wasn't just playing the "Christian role" just to be with me. I wasn't going to force Chris to go to church, or read the bible with me because he needed to desire God for himself. That's why I had to leave Chris alone with God. For months, we were apart with no communication, but during that time God was working on us individually, fruit was growing on both our ends before the season came for us to be married. Like mentioned previously, Chris got planted in a local church, was studying the bible, got saved, baptized, spoke in tongues and actually lived the life, and didn't just pretend to.

Even though Chris and I didn't communicate, I would still talk to his cousin occasionally. From time to time she would update me on his walk with Christ and I truly believe God gave me her as a source to actually see the fruit being produced in his life without interfering with the situation. During that time, I had to break off bad relationships as well, cut off all ties with my ex, overcome lust and develop a mind of purity and modesty. This had to happen in order for me to be prepared for our courtship and engagement, in which we had boundaries.

"By their fruit you will recognize them. Do people pick grapes from thornbushes, or figs from thistles? Likewise, every good tree bears good fruit, but a bad tree bears bad fruit. A good tree cannot bear bad fruit, and a bad tree cannot bear good fruit. Every tree that does not bear good fruit is cut down and thrown into the fire. Thus, by their fruit you will recognize them." – Matthew 7: 16-20

"Does "The One" even exist?"

For a while, there's been a big debate on whether or not there is such thing as "The One." I would like to address this topic, not with my mere opinion, but with evidence from the scripture. I would also like to explore this idea of "The One" from many different angles because people can look at this with different perspectives.

When people think of "The One," they think of someone who was specifically designed to be their "soul mate." Or, you may have heard the phrase, "my other half" used in conversations about "The One". There is this universal perception that "The One" is someone who is supposed to complement you in a romantic relationship, or even complete you.

Because of this widespread idea, many people go around feeling empty, incomplete, as if a very crucial part of their life and very being is missing. They listen to society that feeds them the lie that when they find "The One", when they find that special person, they will live happily every after. This idea has become so engrained within the general population, that women now naturally have a desire for a "Cinderella story" or a fairytale. Everyone is looking for their "prince charming."

Now, do I believe that God places specific people in our lives to serve a specific purpose? Yes. Do I believe that God can hand pick your spouse for you and actually lead you to His best? Yes. Now, do I believe that the person you end up getting married to will be "The One?" No.

I say no because, this idea surrounding "The One" and the expectations placed on "The One" are impossible for any single man on this earth to fulfill. The good news is, "The One" does exist… the revelation is that, "The One" is not any man on this earth, but *The One* is Jesus Christ. Can you believe that so many of us have spent years, lots of money, and sacrificed so much to find that "One" when the true One has been right in front of us the whole time, just waiting for the day that we'd acknowledge Him and accept His free gift. Just waiting for the moment that we'd notice Him, cast our cares upon Him, and trust Him to meet our every need rather than trusting in a man.

Sis, you may have spent all these years looking for a husband, but did you know that God is your husband? This is not just a cool spiritual saying. If you really look deep down and meditate on that truth and realize, that you are married to the Creator of the universe, the Creator of your soul, you would be amazed at how much that truth would set you free. God is your soul mate. When you die and leave this earth, your soul is not going to unite with any other man on this earth, you soul will either go to heaven or hell, and if you take the time to develop this relationship with Jesus now, that place will be heaven, where you soul will be united with the true Prince forever. Who cares for a prince charming when you can have The Prince of Peace and King of kings?

Being a married woman has given me the revelation, that my husband is not my soul mate and he is not "The One" for me. Don't get me wrong. I love my husband so much and I'm happy in our marriage, but my husband was not created to carry that type of burden and expectation. Only God could fill that empty void I had in my heart. I can be away from my husband for a week and even though I would miss him greatly, my soul can still be filled with pure joy, I will still be whole. I cannot say the same about God. When, I don't spend even a day with God, I feel lonely, irritated, empty, and even sometimes depressed.

You see, God is the lover of my soul. He is The One who came to this earth and died for my soul... purchased my soul from hell so that I could spend eternity with Him. There is no other soul mate for me. There is no other One that could lead me to salvation, to an eternity of bliss besides Jesus. John 14:6 says:

"Jesus answered, "I am the way and the truth and the life. No one comes to the Father except through me."

75

Sis, if you think that marrying someone, no matter how "perfect" they look, is going to complete you, you are sadly mistaken. All of us are but mere dust, and dust we will return. It is not fair for us to place such high expectations on any man. I am not saying not to have standards, and I am not saying to go on and be with any fool... but no one else on this earth can love you like God loves you.

Our life is but a mist, God forbid you marry someone, and the next day they pass away due to a horrific tragedy. Will that be the end of your life? And if you thought they were "The One" does that now mean that there is no one else you can ever be with? Then are you going to be angry at God and say, "Why did you take this person away from me!" Beloved, God gives and God can also take away. It was not His will in the first place for us to put someone in a position that was only meant to be for Him. I don't mean to sound insensitive and I know that in those situations it can really hurt, but we have to talk about it.

I even asked myself this question, "If my husband died today, could I go on with life?" I would mourn, I would cry, but I am so happy that I know there's a hope beyond this life of pain and misery. To this day I look forward to the return of my eternal Prince, my King, and my Groom Jesus Christ. I want to be ready. I don't want to be so consumed with my life now and my relationships and idols now, that I forget that there's another wedding I have to attend one day. Jesus is coming back for His bride. He's coming back for me, and I am patiently and hopefully waiting in expectation. I don't place my hope in anything or any man on this earth. My hope is in Him and Him alone.

Because of that, my marriage has been transformed. When I remembered that my husband wasn't "The One," and God was, I was able to lend more grace to him. I get to focus on the purpose that my husband and I have together as a couple, and the reason why the Lord put him in my life. I get to love him more and nag him less because I know he's not perfect and I don't expect him to be. Our marriage has grown so much because the central focus is no longer, "how can I change this person and turn them into someone who meets my every need" to "How can I be a better wife to truly love this person and bring God glory through my marriage."

Now when I act in love, even when I know my husband may not deserve it, I do it as unto God... because I know that God is my Husband and I'm the one who doesn't deserve Him. I don't deserve His grace, His love, His forgiveness, His patience, but He gives it anyway. He chose to marry me anyway! *Me God? In all my rags and dirt? Me Jesus? Creator of the whole universe? You want to spend eternity with me?* Talk about hitting the jackpot!

Sis, you don't have to keep waiting on "The One" to come along. The One is here, with you, right now, today. Waiting for you to run back to Him, He waits with open arms. He is here to wipe away every tear, wash you with His word, and love you back to life. This is what you've been looking for, all along.

"Do not be afraid; you will not be put to shame. Do not fear disgrace; you will not be humiliated. You will forget the shame of your youth and remember no more the reproach of your widowhood. For your Maker is your husband—the LORD Almighty is his name—the Holy One of Israel is your Redeemer; he is called the God of all the earth. The LORD will call you back as if you were a wife deserted and distressed in spirit—a wife who married young, only to be rejected," says your God. For a brief moment I abandoned you, but with deep compassion I will bring you back. In a surge of anger I hid my face from you for a moment, but with everlasting kindness I will have compassion on you," says the LORD your Redeemer." – Isaiah 54:4-8

Finally, seeing God as my husband, and seeing how He took me in and loved me unconditionally, despite the fact I had been running all my life, is what made me content in my season of singleness. I wasn't thirsty for a husband, because I knew who my Husband was, and he was able to quench any type of thirst I had. Jesus said to her,

"Everyone who drinks this water will soon become thirsty again, but whoever drinks of the water that I will give him will never be thirsty again. The water that I will give him will become in him a spring of water welling up into eternal life."- John 4:14

I changed the well I was drinking from. I realized that the well of relationships I had used to quench my thirst was only temporary, and I realized God's well was eternal. Marriage on earth is "till death do us part", but our marriage with Jesus is forever and ever.

"And I am convinced that nothing can ever separate us from God's love. Neither death nor life, neither angels nor demons, neither our fears for today nor our worries about tomorrow—not even the powers of hell can separate us from God's love. No power in the sky above or in the earth below—indeed, nothing in all creation will ever be able to separate us from the love of God that is revealed in Christ Jesus our Lord." - Romans 8:38-39

So no, my Sister, despite what you've been through regarding relationships and marriage, your hope isn't lost. There is a hope that no man or devil in hell could ever take away from you, and that hope is in Jesus. In due season, you will recognize your earthly husband, because he will look like Jesus. In his character, in his love, in his actions, you will recognize the fruit. You'll be so caught up in your love affair with God that, when the time comes, you will be caught by surprise. And the only reason that man will even get the slightest bit of your attention is because he will look familiar, he will remind you of a love you've already known, he will remind of your spiritual husband, Jesus.

"And now, Lord, what do I wait for? My hope is in you."
- Psalm 39:7

Now that we know who *The One* is, we can talk about this idea of God revealing to you your future husband with the proper perspective. We know that our future husband on this earth won't be *The One* but that doesn't mean they aren't in our life for a purpose. Marriage is all about purpose. So what does the bible say about purpose and pre-destination? We must consider this because, based on what the bible says, we will be able to determine how our future/current spouse, fit's into the picture.

The bible says in Jeremiah 29:11 (KJV), "For I know the thoughts that I think toward you, saith the LORD, thoughts of peace, and not of evil, to give you an expected end." I love how that verse ends with an "expected end". God is not surprised by your life and circumstances. He knows all things. God has a specific plan for your life. Jeremiah 1:5 says, "Before I formed you in the womb I knew you, before you were born I set you apart; I appointed you as a prophet to the nations." Not a second that passes in your life takes God by surprise, not one. God has a plan for you, and so does the enemy. But God is all-powerful, He knows the enemy's plans, He can read the enemy's thoughts. No matter how sly the enemy is or how secretive he tries to be, God is always millions of steps ahead of him.

God has already ordained multiple open doors of escape for every one entrapped by the enemy. That's why the bible says: "No temptation has overtaken you except what is common to mankind. And God is faithful; He will not let you be tempted beyond what you can bear. But when you are tempted, he will also provide a way out so you can endure it." (1 Corinthians 10:13) God is saying, whatever you're going through, many people in the past, present, and future, have gone or will have gone through the same thing. Not only that, but he, the same God who helped those people get through those similar struggles, is the same God with you today and every day of your life.

God is omnipotent. Do you know what that means? According to dictionary.com, as an adjective, the word omnipotent is defined as almighty or infinite in power, as God. I love how they said "as God". He is the example for omnipotence because He is the only omnipotent One. His power is defined as infinite, meaning it's never ending. Sit and think about it. Take at least a minute to think of God's power like a long line just growing and growing and growing and never stopping over time. It will blow your mind.

God knows *all* things. When I say all, I literally mean all. Even the things we overlook. Even the things we consider mundane and unimportant. He knows of them. God handles His creation with care. To truly care for something, you must have knowledge about it. For instance, you won't be able to care properly for a newborn child if you don't learn about them personally, and about what can help them and what can hurt them. For example, you have to know you can't leave little things lying around on the floor when a baby starts crawling. In the same way, God cares for us, but to a more extreme level. He not only knows what's best for us, He knows us better than we even know ourselves. He created us, each uniquely and differently; even identical twins are created with a unique personality, purpose, and journey. No two people are the same. I believe God did this for a reason. God wanted to express His love for us by making all of us different. He wants to show you He is willing to know you and love you as you are.

Really, think about it. Imagine a world where everyone was the same. Imagine if God wasn't the same God, if he wasn't a creative God, but just a lazy god, instead of an omnipotent God, just a simple god. He wouldn't take the time out to make billions of people and have each of them be different. We'd all have the same name, the same height, the same hair, the same eyes, the same everything. There would be no need for family because we would all belong so ourselves. All the same, but also separate. We'd be separate and alone because we wouldn't need each other. There would be no one else in this world that had anything you didn't have. No one would need you and you wouldn't need anyone. Everyone would be the same and would be purposeless and insignificant, just another spot on this earth amongst billions of other people.

The enemy may try to lie and tell you you're not special. He tries to tell you God doesn't care about you or that He's forgotten about you. Are you kidding me? That is so not true! Every single part of who you are was birthed from a thought and word from God. Everything. The family you were placed in, the neighborhood you grew up in, the gifts and talents you have; God designed all of those things for a purpose.

He gave you something someone else doesn't have, so when you come together with that person, a need would be met. He may have given you a loving heart, because someone else's life is filled with hate. When your light meets their darkness, there is a spiritual explosion that happens and that explosion is the glory of God. Who we are, the reason we're here, everything is for the glory of God. That's why we are instructed:

"So whether you eat or drink or whatever you do, do it all for the glory of God."-1 Corinthians 10:31

Now that we have addressed God's ultimate design for life and purpose, we can see that, yes, there can be such a thing as God having a spouse in mind specifically for you, in the proper context. That context being: if God has actually destined for you to be married. Also, if the person He has for you is in the context of His will and purpose for your life, not outside of it. So if you so choose to walk in the enemy's purpose for your life, instead of God's, you very well may miss out on that person—and yes, you do have a choice, even in the midst of God's omnipotence. It's a paradox.

"This day I call the heavens and the earth as witnesses against you that I have set before you life and death, blessings and curses. Now choose life, so that you and your children may live." - Deuteronomy 30:19

Now, keep in mind, to be outside of God's will, you have to be sinning against God and denying Him. If you are making a conscious effort to pursue God and your heart is pure, grace will pull you back in whenever you begin to stray off of the course God has for you.

For example, when I first met Chris, I was in a season of backsliding. We didn't start by doing everything right, but God had allotted a certain amount of grace for me in that season. That grace wasn't there so I could continue to drift away and use the excuse, "Well, God's got me." Grace was there so I could be drawn back into God's presence without having to go back and start from scratch. Grace lets you continue on the path right where you left off so you don't have to get saved again and again at the altar call every Sunday. Grace says, "come as you are".

By God's grace, I took a break from the toxic relationship I had with Chris when we first met and I got closer to God and refocused my attention on Him. When I got back on the path God had planned for me, and Chris was on his path, God worked on us individually and then brought us together for marriage in His perfect timing. Our testimony and relationship ended up brining glory to God, but get this—if I had kept going down the wrong path, quenching the voice of the Holy Spirit and actively choosing to disobey God, I would've walked outside of my purpose. If I had married Chris at that point, he would no longer be the spouse that God had for me and our relationship would not bring God glory.

So Karolyne, you're saying the same person who could be God's choice for you in one instance, may not be His choice in another? Yes, that's exactly what I'm saying. What you need to understand is, God destined for me to be married to the saved Chris, not the worldly Chris. Though he may seem like the same person in the world's eyes, he's not the same person to God. When you get saved, you put on the new man. You really are not the same person anymore because your whole identity has changed.

You see, today that person may not be meant for you and they may never be. Or, today they may not meant for you but tomorrow they might be. Let me be clear that I am talking about the process of knowing the proper spouse BEFORE marriage. After you tie the knot, you should stay with that person because God hates divorce, so work it out. That's why it's so important to be led by God and to have an intimate relationship with Him. He'll tell you when it's time to wait, when it's time to go.

We feel like, just because God revealed our husband, we need to go up to him and tell him and be together now! Sister, if that man really is supposed to be your husband in the future, and God has chosen to reveal him, pray. Pray for his heart, pray for his soul, and pray for his leadership. The more you obsess over the guy and become distracted, the more you prolong the process because he won't be growing as fast as he could be growing in order to take the step to pursue you one day. If you truly believe God has revealed your future husband to you, and you want the process to be graced and bring glory to God...pray for this man! You don't know what it is the Lord could be working in him, preparing him for, or what he could be going through.

At one point before we were married, I remember taking to Chris' cousin and referring to him as my husband. She responded with something along the lines of, "No, he's your future husband." That convicted me so much. She was right. I was getting ahead of myself. I was so excited, that even before the wedding day, I was calling Chris my husband when the reality of the matter was he wasn't my husband yet. When I humbled myself and changed my mindset, it actually helped me remain pure throughout our courtship and engagement.

At a time where we were trying our best to stay pure, Chris brought up this awesome way to look at it. He said, "You are not my wife yet. If I do anything with you now, I will be cheating on the married version of you with the engaged you and you may not be happy about it later."

Looking at it that way really placed a righteous fear and conviction in our hearts. During our engagement, when things got heated, I'd was able to look at Chris and think, I respect you, but I respect my husband so much more, I wouldn't want to do anything with you that would take away from the experience I have with you has my husband later. We wanted to protect our purity for our future selves because we knew marriage meant forever, divorce was out of the question, and the lustful desires we couldn't act upon at that moment were only temporary. We wouldn't want to taint something for a lifetime, in a quick five minutes. It just wasn't worth it.

Now listen, don't let the enemy condemn you; there is no condemnation in Jesus. You don't have to feel like there's no hope for you if you've already gone through that phase and you didn't exactly do it the right way. Or if you married someone who was unsaved and now you feel like you married the wrong person, there is still hope. The past is erased and long gone. Do you remember what I said about God's grace? It's there to pull you back in if you've gotten off track and help you move forward. If your heart is willing to change and if you truly desire to bring God glory, repent, turn from your ways, and realize God is standing there with open arms, ready to receive you. This grace is available to anyone.

When you have a true encounter with God's love just once, you wont want to go back. His love is so amazing! You have to be in some serious bondage to experience God's love and His presence and still pursue destruction full force. Remember, God provides a way out of everything. Even if you feel like you've married the wrong person, even if you didn't do things right in the beginning, there is still hope.

"And we know that all things work together for good to them that love God, to them who are the called according to his purpose." - Romans 8:28

If God designed everything with purpose and He designed marriage with a purpose of being a reflection of Christ's relationship with the church, why would He skip over the detail of designing someone specifically for you to embark on that journey with? The reason people are trying to convince others that God can't do this or won't do that, is because of their need for control. They have a lack of faith in God's sovereignty and because of this, they are afraid that God may not have everything under control. They don't want to rely on God's best choice for them so they take matters into their own hands.

Like I mentioned before, free will does play a role in God's design because God did not make us robots. He made us human beings with feelings, emotions, our own wills and convictions. It is up to us to trust God and seek the Holy Spirit's leading for guidance when it comes to choosing a spouse... we have the freedom to choose of course, but why wouldn't you want to go to the One who has the best choice in mind?

People rely heavily on finding a spouse through dating networks, because those networks have a large database of people that could match them with someone else that is compatible... but God has access to the largest database, it's called the universe! Almighty God knows every single man on the face of this earth and He knows each and everyone one personally and intimately. He hears their thoughts, sees their hearts, and knows their qualifications.

It's honestly a waste of time to try and take matters into our own hands when we can get the best possible results by just trusting God to choose are spouse. He knows us and the other person, and what we both need. He knows how two people will complement one another. Believe me, if you are willing to let God choose a specific person on the earth just for you, He will be more than happy to do it. So no, we are not robots, and yes we can choose anyone we want, but why not care to know if God has a preference?

If we are actually living for God this will all happen naturally, despite our own free will. God has the power to shape our circumstances, so if were in Him, in many ways our decisions are influenced by Him regardless. When we are in His will, our free will lines up with His just as our desires become His desires. So yes, we make our choice. We fall in love with someone and we get to know him or her, but

God had that choice in mind to begin with. When you choose the right spouse for you, that does not make you sovereign over your life and you do not get the credit, you are just acting in agreement to the sovereign One's plan for your life.

God did not send any random man to be the Messiah and die on the cross. It had to be Jesus. It had to be His one and only son, God in the flesh. Jesus was the perfect man for the task. He was humble, He was obedient, He was holy, loving, and determined. He was about His Father's business and just as God takes His business seriously, Jesus took His assignment seriously. God goes all out! I'm so happy that God chose who our Savior would be, and not us. We may have chosen some celebrity or political figure, and if that was the case, I know for a fact we wouldn't have the gift of salvation that we have today.

God thinks things out, He puts people in our lives to fulfill a specific purpose and He can see the implications down the road, both good and bad. God is not going to say He has a purpose for your life and then put in minimal effort. He wants the best for you because He knows what's best, just like Jesus was the best possible choice for the church. Don't let people fill your mind with new philosophies and ideologies nowhere based in scripture. If you seek the root of the argument, many times it is based in doubt. How can you believe something stemming from doubt? The words "believe" and "doubt" do not belong in the same sentence. You have to understand who God is and really understand His design for life to answer many of the blurry questions we ask today. The answers are there, you just need to be willing to believe it.

Finding Hope After Losing "The One"

So what happens if the person we thought was "The One" is no longer there? What happens if we are separated from that special person through death or tragedy? How do we cope? How do we recover? Do we go out and find someone else? Do we just accept it and live the rest of our lives mourning the loss? Can there be someone else out there for us?

Losing your significant other can be extremely hard. Especially if you don't feel like you've had an adequate amount of time to spend with him or her. Our life is but a mist that appears and vanishes in a moment (James 4:14). It seems as if there are many events in our life we have no control over, and it's true. We can't bring that person back no matter how hard we try, and even if we blame ourselves repeatedly for their passing, more times than not, it was truly a circumstance we couldn't control. It may have been sickness, disease, old age, or sudden death… but regardless, God has the final say.

Yes, in Jesus, we have the authority to heal the sick, cast out demons, and so on but what happens when you pray for that person until your head hurts but God still allows them to die? Do you curse God and die internally? Or do you continue to believe in His perfect plan, knowing nothing takes Him by surprise?

In the bible, Job was faced with a similar dilemma; he was being tempted and tested by the enemy. Many would wonder and question, why God would allow such a righteous man to endure such hardship from the hand of the enemy. God gave Satan permission to inflict Job with sores throughout His whole body. Job was challenged by his very own wife who, according to Job 2:9, said, "Are you still maintaining your integrity? Curse God and die!" He had a decision to make. In times of hardship, in the midst of having lost so much, would he comply with his wife's suggestion, or would he continue to trust God? He replied, "You are talking like a foolish woman. Shall we accept good from God, and not trouble?" In all this, Job did not sin in what he said. (Job 2:10)

In life we may go through our own Job experience. Sometimes, God will allow things to happen that we don't want to accept or don't necessarily enjoy. I say the word "allow" because when we are children of God and submitted under His lordship, the enemy can't touch us without His permission. One of these questions in your mind may be, *Why? Why God? Why would you allow this to happen? Why would you allow me to go through this? Why would you give me this life and take it away? Why would you give me this relationship and take it away?* Job, being a mere man like us, questioned God as well in Job Chapters 38-41, which I recommend you read. God responds to Job and he begins,

> "Who is this that obscures my plans with words without knowledge? Brace yourself like a man; I will question you, and you shall answer me. Where were you when I laid the earth's foundation? Tell me if you understand. Who marked off its dimensions? Surely you know! Who stretched a measuring line across it? On what were its footings set, or who laid its cornerstone – while the morning stars sand together and all the angels shouted for joy?" - Job 38:2-7

God was reminding Job of His sovereignty. God was not surprised by Job's situation and as the God who planned the entire existence of our universe, from its foundation to every last tiny cell in our bodies; surely God had a plan for Job and for his life.

The bible says, in Job 42: 10-17:

> "After Job had prayed for his friends, the Lord restored his fortunes and gave him twice as much as he had before. All his brothers and sisters and

everyone who had known him before came and ate with him over all the trouble he Lord had brought on him, and each one gave him a piece of silver and a gold ring. The Lord blessed the latter part of Job's life more than the former part. He had fourteen thousand sheep, six thousand camels, a thousand yoke of oxen and a thousand donkeys. And he also had seven sons and three daughters. The first daughter he named Jemimah, the second Keziah and the third Keren-Happuch, Nowhere in all the land were there found women as beautiful as Job's daughters, and their father granted them and inheritance along with their brothers. After this, Job lived a hundred and forty years; he saw his children and their children to the fourth generation. And so Job died, and old man and full of years."

It's okay to mourn during a crisis, but it's not God's will for us to stay there forever. Psalms 30:5 states, "For his anger lasts only a moment, but his favor lasts a lifetime; weeping may stay for the night, but rejoicing comes in the morning." Job was a very blessed man before the enemy tested his life. But as we read, the Lord blessed Job more in his latter than before the storm. The same God who laid the foundations of the earth, the same God who doesn't skip over details, is the same God who had a plan B for Job's life. Because Job didn't curse God and die, because he humbled himself and let God be God in his situation, he was able to see plan B. But some of us are so angry about how plan A ended; we don't even give God an opportunity to work in our life. So we live in the in-between. The in-between is where the enemy is—tormenting us. It's there in that in-between hallway where he feeds us the lie that our life is over, that it will never get better from this point on. That's not true. If you've accepted the lie, that's what's keeping you from plan B. Don't accept the lie—accept the promise.

There is a rainbow after the storm. There is joy in the morning. God is not surprised by your life and He does have a plan for you. You can love again. You can love even more. Your flesh won't let you believe it because the pride within you says things need to be done a certain way. The pride in you says your life and your journey has to look like everyone else. But God has a funny way of interrupting our plans and dreams. He has a way of not meeting our expectations, but superseding them.

If you end up getting married a second time in life, you may not have the same love for that person, as you did for the first, but you can still love. The first person wasn't "The One" and the second person won't be "The One" either but God had a specific plan for your first marriage, and if it's his will for you to be married again, He will also have a specific plan for your next. Don't lose hope; the best is yet to come!

"*I think I married the wrong person*"

So what happens when you end up in a marriage with the person you thought was "The One" and times begin to get tough? There may be different aspects of that person you discover you don't like, and never knew were there. You may even ask yourself, *who is this person?* And your natural instinct may make you wonder if you made a mistake in marrying them.

As humans, when times get rough, many of us are quicker to find excuses and explanations rather than solutions. One of the reasons why it's so important to keep God first in your relationship, is because you will need the Holy Spirit to guide you in your marriage and communicate what steps to take when times get hard. Your prayer life needs to be strong and you need to be in constant connection with God because the enemy hates marriages.

The devil hates marriage because of the very purpose behind it. Marriage is a ministry, it reminds us of the love Jesus has for us (His bride). So much, that he laid down his life for us. It reminds us of His promise— he has gone to prepare a place for us and He is returning soon (John 14:3). The devil hates that. Don't be fooled, he knows the bible, he knows of God's promise and he wants to do everything he can to turn people away and distract them from God's plan. He has and will continue to go to great lengths to create division in our marriages and in our families because he knows our relationships are the foundation of our community, the foundation of our church and oneness in Christ. He wants us to get used to being in divisive environments and arguments so we can never come together and fulfill the purpose of Christ.

The enemy will throw thoughts in your mind and make you question your marriage so you feel you have an excuse to give up. But the bible is very clear, God hates divorce (Malachi 2:16) and it even encourages those who are unequally yoked in their marriage to stay together. This does not mean to marry someone who you are unequally yoked with, especially since you have the knowledge it is wrong and doing wrong when you know what's right is a sin (James 4:17). The message of not being unequally yoked is about making the best decision prior to ending up in a marriage with someone.

So what happens if you get married before coming to the knowledge of Christ? Maybe you or your spouse didn't do everything exceptionally right in the beginning, but then one of you gets saved in the marriage and the other is not. Even in this case, the bible does not call for divorce. You can't say you think you married the wrong person just because they aren't serving God the way you want them to, praying, or worshipping the way you'd like, and then want to divorce them. I encourage you to pray for your spouse and not nag them, because God can change their heart and it's God's goodness that leads men to repentance (Romans 2:4). Take heed to the scriptures below:

"And if a woman has a husband who is not a believer and he is willing to live with her, she must not divorce him. For the unbelieving husband has been sanctified through his wife, and the unbelieving wife has been sanctified through her believing husband. Otherwise, your children would be unclean, but as it is, they are holy. But if the unbeliever leaves, let it be so. The brother or the sister is not bound in such circumstances; God has called us to live in peace. How do you know, wife, whether you will save your husband? Or, how do you know, husband, whether you will save your wife?" - 1 Corinthians 7:12-16

Ask yourself, why is it you think you married the wrong person? Is it because, as it turns out, they didn't actually fit everything on your list? Do you feel as if they don't understand you? Are you comparing your marriage to other marriages around you and to those glamorized on social media? Seriously, you need to ask yourself why because we tend to go through our whole life with an image in our head of how we expect marriage to be or how we want our marriage to look, and when it doesn't turn out the way we expect, we want to run, we want to blame our spouse, we want to go back on our vows and forget all the confirmation we received before we got married and say maybe I married the wrong person or maybe it was a mistake or maybe I didn't really hear God.

If you give up now, I guarantee you will never be able to witness what God can do in your marriage. You will never experience how others will be blessed and changed, maybe even saved by your marriage ministry later down the road. You have to stick it through. You have to start praying for your spouse and stop complaining and gossiping about them. You have to start passing those tests and allowing some fruit to grow on your tree. What about patience? What about submission? What about respect and true unconditional love, even when we don't feel like our spouse deserves it? I'm telling you; I've been there.

Honestly, I've gotten to some dark and hopeless points in my marriage and I've asked the question, "God, did I make a mistake?" But the Holy Spirit reminded me of how He used to counsel and teach me how to deal with my relationship and spouse throughout courtship and engagement, and He is the same Holy Spirit who is able to lead me now. He is same Holy Spirit who would tell me things as specific as what to say to my spouse, how to love him; and the same Holy Spirit who would tell me to trust my husband to lead us, even though I didn't always agree and understand—but I had to get into my prayer closet. The very fact that God gives me advice on how to work through my marriage and how to deal with my husband just goes to show it is His will for me to stay and work it out.

In the bible, there is scripture after scripture of how we should be in our marriages, how we should be in our relationships. We have no excuse to leave our failing marriages and relationships, if we haven't spent time in prayer. We have no excuse to leave if we haven't spent time reading the word and actually applying those principles to our daily living.

Many of us know what the bible has to say, we know what we should do, but we don't do it. The real challenge is in applying what we learn and passing the tests that come our way. We know to be patient, we know not to nag, but the real challenge is when we're in the moment and our spouse does something that incites such a rage inside of us, we have the option to retaliate, or redirect the situation. You can either try to get back at your spouse, or you can turn the situation toward a place of love and compassion. Remember, you're not supposed to be fighting against your spouse. You both are in this together.

In our marriages, God is calling us to love unconditionally, meaning, even though our minds try to change about our spouse tomorrow, our love shouldn't change. Even though things don't go the way we expect them to, our love should remain. It is not our job to judge our spouse and deem them as not good enough, not romantic enough, not holy enough. Jesus did not do that to us when He died on the cross. He didn't say, "These people are not worthy enough, not thankful enough, not holy enough so I will not die for them... they don't deserve me, I am the Son of God, they are merely sinful men." What if Jesus had said that? None of us would be saved. Instead, the bible says in Romans 5:8,

"But God demonstrates his own love for us in this: While we were still sinners, Christ died for us."

Are we ready to demonstrate this type of unconditional love? Though our spouse is still imperfect; will we still die to ourselves? While our spouse still leaves their socks on the floor, will we still pick them up? While our spouse still doesn't show appreciation, will we still make them dinner? If the question of your spouse and your entire marriage is coming from a place of judgment, you need to get your eyes off of your spouse and start putting your eyes on you. When I took my eyes off of Chris, stopped questioning him and everything I thought he did wrong, God was able to change me and that in turn inspired my own husband to change in many ways and my marriage started to progress, develop, and grow for the better.

"Wives, in the same way submit yourselves to your own husbands so that, if any of them do not believe the word, they may be won over without words by the behavior of their wives, when they see the purity and reverence of your lives."

– 1 Peter 3:1-2

"What about arranged marriages?"

Did you know that arranged marriages have a lower divorce rate and are many times more successful than what we consider to be "love marriages"? According to a University of Florida website (iml.jou.ufl.edu), "Low divorce rates in countries with arranged marriages points to the success of the arranged marriage. High divorce rates in countries with love marriages indicate that perhaps this form of marriage does not work."

With that being said, in free countries like America, where we have the freedom to marry whomever we please, many are looking for a solution to lower the divorce rate and fix broken marriages. I think it would be interesting to see how the divorce rate would be influenced if we let God "arrange" more of our marriages. If parents, mere humans, in some countries can arrange marriages for their children while looking out for their best interest, and have those marriages be successful, what more could we get out of letting our heavenly Father have such involvement in our relationships? Just an idea to ponder...

According to the same website, a man named Dr. William Cornell, a marriage counselor and professor, explained the perspective of an arranged marriage. He claims, "In an arranged marriage, you love the person who is in that position. So, you love your wife because she is your wife, and because she is the mother of your children." I find this statement interesting because God loves us in a similar fashion.

God does not love us because we do everything perfect, He loves us because we are His children, His creation, and nothing can change that. In my own marriage, I don't believe I should divorce my husband because he doesn't do everything I want. We don't always see eye-to-eye. But because I know God arranged my path in such a way where I ended up marrying my husband, it's His will I stay married, grow to love my spouse, and work through it despite our differences.

I believe people in arranged marriages grow to understand unconditional love in its truest sense because it was never based on passion; mere lust was not the foundation of their union, and marriage was something bigger than they were. It wasn't just about their feelings and how that person would cater to their needs. The marriage was arranged with consideration of how the rest of the family would be influenced, their future lineage, and so on. God is not just trying to give you a husband to make you feel good. Marriage is more than that. He's thinking of how your marriage will influence your family, the body of Christ. What type of lineage will your marriage leave behind? What type of assignment and purpose will you fulfill and how will others be impacted through your marriage?

Even though marriages in America and other democratic countries are considered "love" marriages, I believe it's the worldly definition of love. Because God is Love and He never fails. Love endures all, and if that's the case, why do so many of these *love* marriages fail so miserably? Half of the marriages taking place nowadays are taking place without God's consent or input and may not even fit His design for marriage. Below is the definition of true love in the bible, and it looks nothing like the foundation upon what many of us base our relationships today.

"Love is patient, love is kind. It does not envy, it does not boast, it is not proud. It does not dishonor others, it is not self-seeking, it is not easily angered, it keeps no record of wrongs. Love does not delight in evil but rejoices with the truth. It always protects, always trusts, always hopes, always perseveres. Love never fails. But where there are prophecies, they will cease; where there are tongues, they will be stilled; where there is knowledge. It will pass away."

- 1 Corinthians 13:4-8

So if you are someone in an arranged marriage or you're from a country where arranged marriages have taken place, don't be discouraged. I know it can seem like everyone in "love marriages" has a freedom you lack or they have more purpose, it is not true. God is still in control, even when it may seem like man is in control. God still has a purpose for you and your marriage. You just have to be willing to put Him first and let Him work through your marriage.

Though you may not agree with everything your spouse does, though you may not even share the same spiritual beliefs and convictions as your husband, you are still called to respect him. You are still called to love him unconditionally. God will not punish you for what you couldn't control or what you didn't know then, but you will be accountable for what you know now.

God is not surprised by your situation and circumstance. Don't get so caught up in the romanticized idea of "love, marriage, and relationships" that you forget you still have a purpose apart from all the roses and uppity emotions. God still has a plan for you and your marriage. Maybe through your marriage and your gentle spirit, your husband will be saved and come to know Christ. And for those who have the freedom to choose, please don't take for granted the opportunity you have to be with someone who shares your values, knows you intimately, and serves your God.

PART TWO:

Enduring The Process Before the Pursuit

"Knowing" Who Your Husband Will Be...

It can be difficult to trust in the Lord sometimes. Trying to have faith in His plan for your life, though sometimes you may be clueless of what that plan is, can be tough for many. On the other hand, sometimes knowing and having to wait patiently for the specific promise given, may seem like the true test.

When we don't know, we may wonder if God will make the right decision. We man even question if He actually knows and recognizes our desires, and fear the uncertainty of how long it may take. Wondering if we'll ever see the day when God's promise will come to pass. Then, for those who do know, the test comes when God has given us a bit of knowledge or insight into a situation. We have two choices:

1. Despite the knowledge we have received, we can choose to deny our own assumptions and natural inclinations to form our own plans.

2. We can decide to take the knowledge we have and try to control and manipulate the situation because we want to make sure what we "feel" God has said, actually comes to pass.

What we sometimes fail to realize is that God does not need our help in keeping His word. He will keep His word all by Himself, whether we are involved or not and whether we have knowledge of the future or not.

"For as the rain cometh down, and the snow from heaven, and returneth no thither, but watereth the earth, and maketh it bring forth and bud, that it may give seed to the sower, and bread to the eater: So shall my word be that goeth out of my mouth: it shall not return unto me void, but it shall accomplish that which I please, and it shall prosper in the thing whereto I sent it." - Isaiah 55:10-11

You can sabotage God's plans for you when you are disobedient and step outside of His will by trying to take matters into your own hands. Here's an example of three different scenarios:

Version #1

Jamie is single, and finally very content in her singleness. She doesn't sit around on the phone talking to her friends about guys and bad relationships and she's not stalking one million couples on Instagram, hoping that one day she'll be like them. In the past, she made marriage an idol. She realized it was bondage; a constant nagging in her head to get married. It was an open door for the enemy to wreak havoc in her life. Finally, she got to a point where she realized she wasn't satisfied. She had an unquenched desire to be married and it was eating away at her. She came to the decision that only Jesus, and not a relationship, a marriage or anyone else could satisfy her. Her prayers changed. She stopped going to God and asking Him to reveal her future. She stopped caring about finding "The One" and got to know the True One. Her focus shifted to Jesus and Him alone.

At times she would get tested and be tempted to get off track and try and seek a husband, but she endured by keeping herself occupied and busy about the Father's business and getting involved at church. She led a women's ministry and started to hold other single ladies accountable in their walk with God. She developed her gifts and passions and eventually started her own catering business, realizing she loved to cook. She didn't even know God was preparing her for her future husband. In her spare time, the Lord instructed her on how to make various meals, wash the dishes, clean her small one bedroom apartment, and she was obedient in the little things.

One day, Jamie had an event to cater to for the leaders of one of the churches in her town. One of the dishes served, was a unique dish Jamie had learned to cook during one of her quiet time with Lord. A man at the event was so overtaken by the delectable taste of that specific dish. He asked the people at his table, "What dish is this? Has anyone tasted anything like it? I must find the one who catered this event." The people at his table agreed that the dish was superb and was like nothing they had tasted before. He took the initiative to find the coordinator of the event, so he could be put in touch with the chef who created the meal that would change his life forever. After the event, the event coordinator introduced this man and Jamie to one another. The man said to Jamie,

"This is, by far, the best creation I have tasted in my entire life. Where did you get your inspiration from?"

"Why, thank you, my Father showed me," Jamie responded.

"Well, I would love to meet such a man. Here's my card," he said as he handed it to her. "I host many events like this around the city and I have one coming up next month. If you would do me the honor of catering at my events, I know many would be blessed by your gift. Also, please invite your Dad."

Over time, Jamie started to cater for these events and developed a friendship with this man. He laughs and they bond when he discovers he and Jamie share the same Daddy. She learns he is a man of God who is kind, loving, and who loves to eat! Eventually, they get engaged, married, and carry out their purpose of ministering about The Bread of Life through meals and messages inspired by God's faithfulness.

Jamie's life changed in a way she never expected. She was on the path God had for her, and so was her future husband. At one point on that path, they were destined to meet. What would have happened if Jamie had been distracted with social media and many different idols in her life? She would've never had those intimate moments with God. She would've never discovered her gift of cooking. She would've never discovered her purpose and, instead of living out God's will and plan for her life, she would be living outside of it. Thankfully enough, God used her past and her history of being distracted and not doing everything right to help encourage and deliver the women she led in her women's ministry group. Many of those women eventually developed a relationship with God as well, and went on to fulfill their own personal destinies. Jamie hadn't known who her future husband would be. At first, she didn't understand her purpose, or know why God was teaching her all the things

He was, but she trusted He had a plan for her life. She rested in this belief and eventually everything came together and worked out perfectly.

Version #2

Jamie is single, and finds it hard to be content in her singleness. She sits around on the phone talking to her friends all day about getting married and stalks a million couples on Instagram, hoping she'll be like them one day. She made marriage an idol and it was bondage in her life. There was a constant nagging in her head to get married. It was an open door for the enemy to enter her life. Finally, she got to a point where she realized she wasn't satisfied. She had an unquenched desire to be married and it was eating away at her. She came to a realization that only Jesus, not a relationship, not a marriage, not anyone else could satisfy her. At one point, her prayers changed. She stopped going to God, asking Him to reveal her future. She stopped caring about "The One" and started getting to know the True One.

Then one day, The Holy Spirit revealed who her husband was and, unknowingly, she went back to her former ways, of worry, of fear, and discontentment. For a little while, she was running a good race, but then she got distracted. She fell back into the habit of comparing her life to everyone else.

"You were running a good race. Who cut in on you to keep you from obeying the truth? That kind of persuasion does not come from the one who calls you." - Galatians 5:7-8

She got involved in women's ministry but instead of going to the meeting to apply the information and make changes in her own life, she went to gossip and talk to other girls who she'd heard God had revealed their husbands to them, too. She filled her time with unfruitful activities instead of being led by God and taking time to hear His voice. She took matters into her own hands, all the while thinking she was preparing to be a wife.

She learned that the man she was supposed to marry went to a different church in her town. He was a leader there and hosted many events for the Christian community. She left her church and went to his because she figured in her mind if he was her husband; she should be at his church instead of trusting God's plans on how they would meet and what church they would eventually attend. At that church, Jamie became friends with many people God never intended her to be friends with. Meanwhile, her home church was teaching a lot of material that could've helped to guide her in that season, but since she wasn't planted where God wanted her to be, she struggled spiritually.

Her new friends were lukewarm Christians and invited her to the club, where she met someone who tried talking to her. She was then confused and questioned whether her husband was who God said he was. She got involved with the man at the club, not recognizing this guy was only a distraction... and her new friends encouraged her relationship rather than keeping her accountable.

She found out one of her friends was a close friend of the family to the guy God revealed was her husband. She saw this as an opportunity to connect with her future husband, so she divulged to her friend that God told her who her husband was. This fake friend took this information and, instead of keeping it confidential, spread the information at a family dinner, in a way that made Jamie come across as crazy and obsessed.

Since it was out of season and out of order and the guy was in a place where God had not spoken to him about Jamie yet, his heart was hardened to this information. He thought: *Who is this girl? She's crazy. God didn't tell me anything about my future wife and, in fact, I've been interested in another woman at church. Maybe she's my wife and this is simply an attack and distraction from the enemy who is trying to get me off track.*

Can you believe that Jamie's disobedience in trying to take matters into her own hands, eventually became a distraction to the man who God had planned her to be a helpmeet to? If she would've trusted in God's promise, instead of trying to fulfill God's promise for Him... she would've spent more time praying for her future husband in different areas, so he could get to the point where the Lord awakened him. She would've stayed at her church and learned what she needed to learn to help her get through that tough season that required much patience. She would've been promoted to be over the women's ministry and freed many women through her testimony and example, but instead, those women were still in their own bondage.

She could've discovered her purpose and gift of cooking. But now she felt purposeless and embarrassed. She could've had a lot of money saved if she'd started a business, and could've put that money towards her wedding, honeymoon, and future marriage, but instead she was in debt. She spent less money on groceries and more money eating out (when she had a gift of cooking), going to the club, fulfilling the lust of the flesh and going on girls' nights with her fake friends, all the while, idolizing marriage all over again.

She continued down this path, not realizing her actions were equated to witchcraft. Not realizing she was out of God's will and outside of His will, the promise no longer applied to her. Two years have passed and she's still single, still discontent, she doesn't even go to church anymore and the man she was supposed to marry moved on. God had a plan B for his life and since he was still walking in God's will and seeking the Lord in all he did, since he loved God and was called according to His purpose, all things worked out for his good, even with his new wife.

Version #3

Jamie is single, and finally very content in her singleness. She doesn't sit around on the phone talking to her friends about guys and bad relationships and she's not stalking one million couples on Instagram, hoping that one day she'll be like them. In the past, she made marriage an idol. She realized it was bondage; a constant nagging in her head to get married. It was an open door for the enemy to wreak havoc in her life.

Finally, she got to a point where she realized she wasn't satisfied. She had an unquenched desire to be married and it was eating away at her. She came to the decision that only Jesus, and not a relationship, a marriage or anyone else could satisfy her. Her prayers changed. She stopped going to God and asking Him to reveal her future. She stopped caring about "The One" and got to know the True One. Her focus shifted to Jesus and Him alone.

Then one day, The Holy Spirit revealed who her husband was and she didn't understand. She sought God in prayer and asked Him, what was the purpose for this? She was ok with being single, but if God had other plans for her, she knew she needed His divine direction and leading. At times she was tested and tempted to get off track to try and manipulate the situation, but she endured by keeping herself occupied and busy about the Father's business and getting involved at church.

She led a women's ministry and started to hold other single ladies accountable in their walk with God. She developed her gifts and passions and eventually started her own catering business, and discovered her passion for cooking. She realized that God was preparing her for her husband so during her time with the Lord, she was intentional about listening to His instructions on how to make various meals, wash the dishes, and clean her small one bedroom apartment, and she was obedient in the little things.

She didn't spend much time with the same friends she had in the past, or go out to eat as much because she knew God was transitioning her into a new season. She was able to save a lot of money during that time, and she opened her own restaurant.

One day, the man who she knew God said would be her husband, walked into her restaurant and ordered her popular dish. He said, "I heard you had the best dish in town, I would like to try it out." Since that day, he fell in love with her food, and returned to the restaurant once a week. At first Jamie began to grow weary. She started to wonder if this man knew who she was, but whenever she would get discouraged, she would go home and pray, and God would reassure her to trust Him.

Then one day, the man told Jamie that he would like to get to know her a little more and asked if they could go out some time. Of course Jamie accepted, and he took her out to an elegant restaurant one lovely afternoon. He immediately laid out his intentions of pursuing her, and let her know that he respects her and if she were interested, would like to court her.

Jamie took some time to pray about it and get back to him, even though she knew he was supposed to be her future husband. She didn't want to risk this precious experience by doing things outside of God's timing, so when she finally got the "go ahead" from God, they began courting. Three months later, they got married and God had been preparing them through prayer, discipline, and being led by his voice before they even got together. What seemed like it was taking forever, sped up at the very end because during the time when Jamie had to wait patiently, even though she knew, she was faithful in waiting and trusting God to work things out.

You see, the most important difference between version 1, 2, and 3 of Jamie was not whether or not God told her who her husband was. Instead, the crucial factor was based on how Jamie responded to being tested in both scenarios. Though the first version of Jamie's life seems perfect, it's only because we are reading the results of her obedience and willingness to stay focused and keep her eyes on God in her season of trusting Him and not knowing who he husband would be. She could have fell back to her old habits and ways. She could have gotten distracted, but she was sincerely changed... not just in her mind but also in her heart and she honestly believed that God was "The One" for her.

Even though it may seem like she had it easier because she didn't know who her husband would be... we have to understand that God sets us up for success and not for failure. Whether God tells you who your husband is going to be or not, know that Him sharing or withholding that information from you is the best thing for you. In whatever case, God is setting us up for success, but how we respond to that set up, determines where we will end up.

If we step outside of the set-up and don't remain still and know that He is God (Psalm 46:10), it's not God's fault. It's simply our bad choice. So even though the second version of Jamie seems as if God had forsaken her, and set her up for failure... that's not the case. Jamie made some bad decisions but God can *still* take those bad decisions and work them out for her good, if she truly loves Him and is called according to His purpose (Romans 8:28). But you can't say you love God and you can't expect Him to work everything out for your good if you don't obey His commands. John 14:15 says:

"If you love Me, you will obey my commands."

God didn't tell the first version of Jamie who her husband would be, because He knew it wasn't the best thing for her. God told the second version of Jamie, because in that case, it was the best thing for her as well, but she made the decision to pursue her desires and be led by her emotions, instead of being led by God.

The second version of Jamie did not seek God in everything; she sought her flesh. She was led by her feelings. She didn't love God and you could tell that by the fruit of her disobedience. She loved the idea of marriage. She was tested and she failed. God did not reveal who her husband was just to tease her, but it was her opportunity to make a decision to pass the test. That's what the third version of Jamie did. She took advantage of the opportunity to rest in Him and in His promises. To prepare in the way He wanted and to grow in prayer, to grow in patience, and to grow in faith.

So if God didn't share with you who your husband is going to be, don't feel like you're less than someone else who knows. Believe that God is making the best decision for you, your life, and future relationship. Your focus should be on Him, developing as an individual, and trusting that He has everything under control. The seeds that you plant now and the decisions that you make will have ripple effect on your life. Make sure it's the kind of ripple effect that you'll actually want to deal with in the future.

If God did tell you who your husband is, don't let that become a distraction. Ask God the reason "why?" because there is purpose in everything He does. One important reason is most likely to just pray for that man... but there may be something specific that God wants you to do in this season and that's "why" He told you. When you shift your perspective and starting working on the "why" and get your mind off of the "when" you'll be able to endure the season with much patience and bear much fruit in the midst.

"We're on a break, is it not meant to be?"

So, you're on a break from the person you thought could potentially be your future husband. When you were together, you were sure of it, but now as distance separates you both and there's a growing silence, you start to wonder if you'll ever be with each other again. You start to wonder if you should wait around, move on, and if that person is really the person you should spend the rest of your life with.

There are several reasons why you may be on a break:

- You both are unequally yoked, so you know it's not the time to be together because you keep falling into sin.

- The person says they have some things they need to work on, "It's not you, it's me" and you feel like you need to wait for them to finish working on themselves.

- Things seem to be getting serious and someone isn't ready for commitment, so they say they need a "break."

- An offense was done in the relationship, someone did something to hurt the other or lose their trust, now you're taking a break to reevaluate and think things through.

The first example is what happened between Chris and me. Initially we played house and put ourselves in tempting situations. I had no standards and no boundaries, but I felt convicted about everything I was doing. Chris didn't feel the conviction because he wasn't saved, so we were unequally yoked. Therefore, God led me to take a break from him, which lasted 7 months.

If we had never pulled away from that situation, we would be spiraling down the wrong path. I don't know if Chris would have gotten saved if we hadn't taken a break. I was a distraction in his life and vice versa. I needed to leave him alone with God so God could work on His heart and His life. I needed to accept that only God could change a man, not me. At the time, I didn't know Chris would be my future husband, so during our break I didn't really have to question if he was still going to be.

If you find yourself asking this question, and you're on a break, my question to you is, "what is your focus?" Maybe the whole point of your break is to help you refocus, take your eyes off that man and keep your eyes on Jesus. So why are you even asking that question? Don't worry about it Sis, if it's meant to be, it'll be.

My break from Chris was about looking into myself and seeing everything I could work on personally, while at the same time letting go of the past and laying down my relationship idols at Jesus' feet. I believe that is the only reason why our break was effective and we were able to come back together. If you are in this situation, but believe the Lord told you this man would be your one day husband before you both went on this break, you have to recognize the purpose of the break. The entire point of the break is to truly separate yourself from this person long enough for them to no longer be a distraction in your life and vice versa.

I love the definitions of break that I found on dictionary.com:

1. To smash, split, or divide into parts violently; reduce to pieces or fragments.

Listen, when God says you need to take a break from someone, it means He wants to do the job of crushing the entire foundation and building it back up from scratch. That is the only way Chris and I were able to come back together as two completely different people than we were before. When we were on our break, we spent time with God to the point of breaking. God weeded so much junk out of our lives and hearts. There was even a point where I was 100% transparent with God for the first time in my life; during my break, I wrote pages upon pages of confessions to the Lord. All my buried sins, all the unspoken things, all the idols, all of the relationships—I even put my relationship with Chris on there. I prayed to the Lord and told Him I surrendered it all to Him. I burnt that paper with fire and asked the Lord to make me free. Can you believe at the end, the fire would no longer light and the only little piece of paper left that had refused to burn said "free"? It was such an overwhelming and memorable milestone. I will never forget it because it was my true moment of brokenness before the Lord. Now I was free to begin again, I was free for God to change my heart and redirect my path.

"Create in me a pure heart, O God, and renew a steadfast spirit within me."–Psalm 51:10

The other definition I found says:

2. To destroy or interrupt the regularity, uniformity, continuity, or arrangement of; interrupt.

Have you ever had God interrupt your plans? Just completely destroy your expectations and take you out of your comfort zone? I have. I've been in an experience matching the last example on the list I mentioned. I was hurt because of an offense that was committed in one of my relationships. As I shared earlier, I was engaged before Chris. This relationship was a longer relationship that started out as a strong friendship. I was honestly convinced that my ex and I would've been together forever—so much time and effort was put into our relationship and I was so comfortable with him. At the time, I told him I couldn't picture myself with anyone else, even after he broke my heart. So though I broke up with him, I still wasn't over him, and we were trying to work things out.

Thankfully, God's interruption of the relationship saved my life. I didn't know it then, but it took me some time to realize it. The Lord had it strategically planned this out; He had a plan of how he would separate us and move me away from that guy forever. I was supposed to leave for college on June 22, 2011, but I chose to stay one more day so I could be home to celebrate my ex-fiancé's birthday. His birthday was the day I got a phone call from a friend who revealed that naked pictures of him had been exposed on social media.

These pictures were ones he'd sent to a girl he called his "best friend". Then it all made sense. No wonder he spent day after day with her and not with me. I would even drop him at her house because I trusted them so much and I was blinded by the situation! You better believe I broke up with him on his birthday. Then, the next day, thankfully I had a nine-hour bus ride to Tallahassee, Florida and far away from him. God knows I needed to get far away because if not, I would've ended up right back in a relationship with him.

I had no standards and my relationship was my idol, plus he lived right down the street from me. It was easy to walk to his house and I could drive there in less than a minute. God was protecting me when He used my schooling to interrupt my plans of eventually marrying this man!

If you are with someone you plan on marrying, and God reveals his heart through a hurtful experience, maybe it's for a reason, Sis? Maybe He's trying to show you something before you step into the wrong marriage with the wrong person. Maybe He's trying to show you that you in fact didn't hear Him correctly and it was the enemy trying to deceive you. Please don't ignore the signs. You are God's daughter and He is going to do what He can to try and protect you, but you need to let Him. There's a difference between a break and a breakup. A break may mean God is rebuilding things to bring them back together, but a break up may mean He is destroying the arrangement altogether. Stop wasting your time fighting God, fighting yourself, and fighting your destiny. Stop trying to force something to be that was never meant to be in the first place.

Now I want to talk about the second example I gave where the person says, "It's not you, it's me" and you're confused about whether you should wait around or not. Sister! Many times men will use this excuse because they are not bold enough to tell you to your face, "No, I don't want to be with you."

I have to be honest. What they are saying may be true and they may have things to work on internally, but it has nothing to do with you and everything to do with them and God. It's not your job to wait for that man. If you do, you're letting him string you along and it's becoming a distraction. The bible says,

"But they that wait upon the LORD shall renew their strength; they shall mount up with wings as eagles; they shall run, and not be weary; and they shall walk, and not faint" -Isaiah 40:31

We should be waiting on the Lord, not on any man to get his act together. If you wait on man and not on the Lord, your result will be the opposite... instead of renewing your strength; you will be feeding your weakness, your weakness of idolizing marriage and relationships over God. Instead of running and not growing weary, or walking and not fainting, you will drain yourself, waiting for the day this man will actually change, waiting for the day when he will man up and finally ask you to marry him.

None of us are perfect, so a guy telling you, "It's not me, it's you, I got to work on myself" is a can of baloney. First, he's being untruthful because it concerns the both of you, not just him. We all fall short. Unless it's a deal breaker—not being saved, being unequally yoked, or living a lifestyle where you are constantly sinning—you should be able to work on yourselves and get through things together.

Chris didn't have it all together when we got married, and neither did I. We had no savings, weren't finished with school and had some basic attitude problems, but we had a heart for God and agreed on putting God first and keeping Him first in our relationship. Because of that, we've been able to work through our imperfections and grow to love each other unconditionally. You will never be the perfect person and have the perfect situation before marriage, but marriage makes you a better person. Your spouse is like a mirror and you get to see parts of yourself you never knew where there and work on those things. Sister, don't let that man string you along, he is missing out. A real man understands the investment he is making when he asks for your hand in marriage. The bible says, "He who finds a wife finds a good thing and obtains favor from the LORD" (Proverbs 18:22). It speaks of your worth. Know your worth; other biblical translations refer to that "good thing" as a "treasure". You are a precious jewel and in due season, the right man won't let you pass him by!

Lastly, if someone is asking for a break and refusing to commit, do yourself a favor and don't take it as a break, it is a break up. Men know what they want. My Pastor, Cornelius Lindsey, says, "Men don't have a problem with commitment, they will commit to their favorites sports teams." It's so true, if they can commit and put on these jerseys they can commit and get you that ring. If they can spend so much time talking about the upcoming game or tournament, they can spend time talking about your future together. If he wants to commit, he will. If not, it just means he isn't completely sold on you; he's just stringing you along in order to appease his own relationship insecurities. Leave that man alone, if he's saying he's not ready to be husband material, believe him.

"*I keep having dreams – what do they mean?*"

So you keep having dreams about this person and you may be thinking: *He has to be the one! I keep getting so many signs and confirmations.* Before you assume he is the "One" because of your dreams, and before you assume all of your dreams actually come from God, let's go over a few points.

Firstly, just because you have a dream from God, it doesn't make it a confirmation. Maybe the dream wasn't from God. So what is the first thing that you do when you get one of these dreams? Do you pray about it? Or do you run to the Internet or your friends? The best interpreter of your dream is the Holy Spirit. Not your friends, everybody else and their mama.

It's also a waste of time to seek dream interpretations without knowing the source of the dream because if the dream isn't from God, I don't really care for an interpretation. A dream from a false source can only lend a false interpretation that adds no profit to my life. That is why the first thing we should do is pray, and in praying, before asking God for the dream interpretation out of anxiety to receive a confirmation, we should ask God if the dream is even from Him and many times we should be able to discern if it is or not.

If you always take your dreams and go to everyone else with them, without every really consulting God, you're setting yourself up for failure because the enemy can use that opportunity to send false prophets into your life to "interpret" the dream he may have given you himself or twist the dream God may have given you, out of context.

> "For the household gods utter nonsense,
> and the diviners see lies;
> they tell false dreams
> and give empty consolation.
> Therefore the people wander like sheep;
> They are afflicted for lack of a shepherd."
> -Zechariah 10:2

Jesus is the good shepherd who lays down His life for the sheep (John 10:11) and apart from Him, apart from the great shepherd, we are lost. If we do not know Jesus, we do not know his voice and we will wander…afflict our own selves because we seek to find a voice we can follow. John 10:27 says, "My sheep listen to my voice; I know them, and they follow me."

Are you spending enough time with Jesus to know His voice and follow Him? If you are, you will be more comfortable and confident going to Him about your dream than to everyone else. Or do you spend more time with your friends and listening to their opinions? Are they your gods?

Really look at your dream. What sticks out? Does anything in your dream represent a symbol or theme presented within or throughout the bible? That's why you must be familiar with your word and reading your word so you know those references, signs, symbols, and metaphors for yourself. The first book we should be running to when we have moments like this is not our "Book of Christian Dreams" some other man wrote, but the bible. I understand, many of us have done it. I have, too before, so I'm preaching to myself! Honestly though, we should run to the bible.

Why aren't we willing to put a little extra time and effort to see what the Holy Spirit would like to show us for ourselves? It's almost as if we are lazy. "Now, now, now, God! I want to know the interpretation now. I want to know if you're saying this is my husband, but I'm so anxious and I don't have time to pray, I don't have time to sit before your feet in silence, I don't have time to go to the word. I will have my answer before you know it if I just enter "Dream Symbols" in an online search!" Sometimes we trust and depend on the Internet more than we do the Holy Spirit, which should not be.

Your dream may even be from you. I minored in Psychology when I went to school and I was able to take a class on dreams and sleep. Granted, I don't believe Psychology is the answer or explanation to everything and sometimes things are simply spiritual, but at the same time, some truth can be found in psychology and it does play a role.

I learned in class that it is very likely for us to dream about anything we're obsessing over in the day, or triggers we may pick up throughout the day because they lie in our subconscious. In spiritual terms, I would translate it as, the manifestation of a seed being planted in your heart. That seed may be a thought you had, a movie you watched, a conversation you engaged in, which became a trigger and open door for the dream.

So, let's say you wake up first thing in the morning, you spend your hour with God and you don't even thank Him for being alive, but you get straight the point. "God please reveal to me, is this my husband?" That man is all you care about and think about and you act as if you have a relationship with God, but you're just using God as a puppet in your selfish scheme. Then you hear your heart say, "Yes, that's your husband" and you think it's the Holy Spirit. You cry, have an emotional moment as if you just heard from God, then your friend calls and you pick up your phone in the midst of spending time with God. How rude. There's no closing prayer, there's no "Thank you, Lord, I'm excited for the day." You hang up on God to pick up the other line because you got your fill and you're ready for your next emotional session. Your friend says,

"Hey girl, what's up? Anything new?"
You tell her God just revealed your husband and you know for sure it is. You talk about how great your time with God was and you come across all holy and deep. You don't even want to know how your friend's day is going or ask if everything is okay with her and you ramble, caught up in yourself.
Your friend asks, "Are you sure? This man doesn't even know you, does he?"
And you say, "Well, just in case it wasn't God and it was me, I am going to pray for some confirmation."

The fact you were able to say that "just in case it was not God" so quickly, shows deep down inside you didn't have peace and you knew it was you trying to make things into what you wanted them to be. It shows you had no business telling anyone "God told me" or "God showed me" because when you really hear from the Lord and you know His voice, you know it's Him even if you try to deny it or don't want to believe it at first.

So, you hang up and pray to God for confirmation. You go through your entire day thinking about the whole situation, wondering when and if God is going to send confirmation. Then you fall asleep and have a dream of you and this man walking down the isle. It wasn't from God and surprisingly enough; it wasn't even from the devil! The devil doesn't even know what's going on with you; he is on the other side of the world causing destruction so don't even blame him.

Those seeds—the pretend time you spent with God, the conversation you initiated with your friend, the thoughts you dwelled on all day—were triggers in your mind and manifested throughout your dream. Now Sis, I don't want to sound harsh, but I have to be real with you because we have to recognize those triggers and open doors we create in our life. If we go throughout life blaming God, the devil, and everyone else without truly evaluating our actions and taking responsibility, we will live a life of confusion because we'll always think we're right and everyone else is wrong. Sister, guard your heart in this season. Guard your heart from what you say, what you think and what you watch. Ultimately what you put in front of you and inside of you, will determine your path. We want to make sure we're putting God's word in front of us, sincere prayer and praise is constantly flowing out of us, and His Holy Spirit is dwelling in us. Not junk.

"Above all else, guard your heart, for everything you do flows from it." – Proverbs 4:23

*"What if he doesn't believe I'm meant
to be his wife?"*

Sis, if a man doesn't believe you're meant to be his wife, most likely, you're not. Please don't waste any time trying to convince him of it. Most men know what they want, especially if they've had the opportunity to spend some time with you. We all have free will. God is not going to force you to be with anyone and He won't force anyone to be with you. The person God has for you will want to be with you because God will place within them that special desire.

Take the testimony of Christian poet and MC, Jackie Hill-Perry, for example. She talks about her past life as a lesbian, and desiring to be with women. She didn't think she could or would ever love or desire to be with a man, but as she aligned herself with the will of God for her life, God grew within her a loving desire for her now husband, Preston Perry, and God protected both of their hearts because they equally desired to be with one another. It is God's job to do the work on the heart. If you feel like that man is supposed to be your husband, maybe it's just not the right time. Maybe he's still blinded to you and the Lord is building up in his heart the desire to love you and notice you as his wife in due season.

Just because he's not paying you the attention you want or engaging with you romantically, does not mean he doesn't believe you're meant to be his wife. Stop jumping to conclusions that result from your wavering emotions and stress during this whole situation. Maybe God has not given him the go ahead to pursue you yet. Maybe there are things he needs to take care of in preparation for when you both come together. If he's busy enough for you to ask the question, "What if he doesn't believe I'm the one?" it just means you're not busy enough! Stop letting that man be a distraction, even if he is your future husband and especially if he's not. It's in God's hands, so give it a rest.

God showed me that Chris was going to be my husband, but I made a decision not to mention anything about it to him. I wanted Chris to grow to love me on his own and share the same goals as me. Not because they were my goals, but because they were his goals and God's plan, and someday they would be our goals. The last thing you want to do is force your goals on a man you believe will be your future spouse. When you do that, you put yourself in a leadership position that was intended for the man in the relationship. You're indirectly telling him, "I hear from God, but you don't. Listen to what God is telling me."

"But I would have you know, that the head of every man is Christ; and the head of the woman is the man; and the head of Christ is God."- 1 Corinthians 11:13

If God says something, it will be accomplished in order. God would not skip over the man, tell you something, and expect you to lead the man on what God told you was supposed to happen. That's not even biblical. God gives us information to help our men lead. We are the helpmeets, not the leaders. We are there to be confirmation, support, that reminder of what God said and promised, especially when times get tough.

The tone that is set in the beginning of the relationship will carry into the relationship. If from the beginning, you coerced this man into marrying you, and he only did so to please you because you're his god or to get in your pants, it will be like pulling teeth to get him to lead later on in the course of your marriage. Then you'll wonder why you feel purposeless, why you both aren't on one accord, why you aren't able to fulfill God's ultimate plan for your marriage. You may not even know that plan because your husband may not have a true genuine relationship with God and may not be able to lead your family. Trust me, you don't want that. Try to get over the uncomfortable "now". Learn to be content in your season because it will lend you the opportunity to truly grow and be prepared for the next.

Now, I believe it is fine for a woman to approach a man because, technically, not everyone who talks to a man is looking for a relationship. There are different reasons a woman may go up to a man and introduce herself. Maybe they are in school and have to work on a project together or she has a question to ask him about the spoken word poem he just recited at a show. I say this to make it clear that I am not presenting a set of laws or actions stating, "This is what you should always do and this is what you should never do."

Honestly, each situation is different and it may not have anything to do with marriage or a romantic relationship. This chapter is not about the suppression of women and I'm not trying to say, "Woman, sit in a corner, hide and don't ever say anything to a man or speak unless you are spoken to." So if God leads you to approach a man for any reason, or it's just a practical part of your daily life, go ahead, introduce yourself and ask what you need to ask or say what you need to say. That's fine! The distinction comes in *pursuing* a man.

Some people get this confused and fall into legalistic actions. To approach a man does not mean to pursue a man. Approaching someone happens in a moment, pursuing someone is a process that develops over time. God did not design women to be the pursuers, but he designed the men to do that. Men are meant to lead. The Hebrew word for "leader" in the bible is *nagid* and it is referred to as a "masculine noun". I'm not saying women can't be leaders. In many areas in life, God will cause women to lead in different situations. I am talking about God's design when it comes to man and woman. In Greek, the word "leader" is *archégos* and is referenced as a masculine noun with the definition: originator, author, and founder. In order for a man to lead and be an originator, he has to start something, not you. Let him get things going and lead the relationship. In order for him to lead and be an author or founder, he has to "find" you. I'm not speaking literal here, but in terms of a relationship. To be found by a man is to be pursued by a man that you accept the pursuit of.

Now I want refer back to the verse that I mentioned previously, and delve a little deeper. Remember, Proverbs 18:22 says, "He who finds a wife finds a good thing and obtains favor from the LORD." It says *he* who finds a wife, not she who finds a husband. This is a reflection of God's ultimate design for a relationship.

I also want to dissect the word "find" because this type of find is not just speaking about a simple game of hide-and-seek. This "find" is referring to the process of pursuing. Part of the process of pursuing, is the search. Before you find someone, you have to be looking for him or her. Ladies, it is not in God's will for you to be looking for any man, but you should be looking for Him. The word "find" in this verse is translated in Greek as *heuriskó* and the definition is: to find, learn, discover, especially after searching. Meaning as leaders and as founders, it is the man's job to find us and as helpmeets, it is our job to be met and someday help meet this man's needs as he continues to lead in the relationship. I love how the definition says, "especially after searching". The search is a major indicator of the pursuit.

"If you keep yourself pure, you will be a special utensil for honorable use. Your life will be clean, and you will be ready for the Master to use you for every good work. Run from anything that stimulates youthful lusts. Instead, pursue righteous living, faithfulness, love, and peace. Enjoy the companionship of those who call on the Lord with pure hearts." - 1 Timothy 2:21-22

I think, as women, it is very important we consider this verse. It tells us the things one should pursue, and nowhere in this verse does it say "a man". It tells us to pursue righteousness, to keep ourselves pure and "companionship with those who call on the Lord with pure hearts" will follow. We wonder why we keep ending up in relationships with people who say they love God, but really don't. We wonder why we end up unequally yoked. We wonder why we end up abused time and time again. It's because instead of pursuing righteousness, we pursued a man. It's because instead of keeping ourselves pure and fleeing youthful lusts, we let our lusts draw us into trouble.

Remember, marriage is not all about me, me, me; God has an assignment He wants accomplished through your marriage. He wants to use your marriage for His glory. Do you see? The verse says, "If you keep yourself pure, you will be a special utensil for honorable use." Any utensil is used for a purpose, but you are more than a utensil, he said you will be a "special" one and you won't just be used for just anything under the sun. God will honor your decision to remain pure during this season; He wants to use you honorably when harvest season comes! But if you're in this season and you're prolonging the process because you're pursuing everything and everyone except God, He's not able to prepare you for the next season. And trust me; God won't let you enter that next season if you're not ready.

You must be ready to be used honorably. When God says He won't give you more than you can bear, this is what He means, Sis. He doesn't mean you'll never face trials; He doesn't mean you'll never face temptation. But are you disciplined? Are you ready for the next level? The grass may look greener on the other side, but it's not green on its own, it takes a lot of hard work, a lot of scorching hot days, mowing the lawn, investing in the proper fertilizer and pesticides. If you can't take care of your own grass, going to the other side won't be any different—you'll have more responsibility, more trials, more tests and you won't be able to handle it. So like a good Father, God is patient with us. He builds us up and He brings on the next season when we're ready. He makes everything beautiful in its perfect time.

1 There is a time for everything,

and a season for every activity under the heavens:

2   a time to be born and a time to die,

a time to plant and a time to uproot,

3   a time to kill and a time to heal,

a time to tear down and a time to build,

4   a time to weep and a time to laugh,

a time to mourn and a time to dance,

5   a time to scatter stones and a time to gather them,

a time to embrace and a time to refrain from embracing,

6   a time to search and a time to give up,

a time to keep and a time to throw away,

7   a time to tear and a time to mend,

a time to be silent and a time to speak,

8   a time to love and a time to hate,

a time for war and a time for peace.

- Ecclesiastes 3:1-8

"He doesn't even know me. Am I crazy?"

So you think God told or showed you who your husband is, but the thing is, he doesn't even know you. Maybe he goes to a different church or lives in a completely different state or country. So many thoughts are constantly clouding your mind and you're probably thinking, *Am I crazy? How will we ever meet? How is he going to know I even exist? Should I take matters into my own hands? should I reach out to him?* and so on.

First, I'm not going to say God wouldn't tell you who your husband is because I'm not God and God can do what He pleases. Second, I'm especially not going to tell you God wouldn't tell you who your husband was if he doesn't know you because, honestly, this just may be the perfect opportunity to exercise your faith. With that being said, I am going to approach this topic from the perspective that maybe God did reveal who your husband is and maybe the man doesn't know about you. There are enough chapters in this book which give examples of different instances where you may have heard God wrong, or instances in which what you say God may have told you doesn't stand in line with His will.

If this is your situation and story, my advice is to trust God in this scenario. Honestly, God is God. If He says He is going to do something, He is going to do it. If you truly believe He has shared this information with you and you've looked at the situation and have complete peace about everything, decide in your heart that you're going to trust Him no matter what.

Distance is not going to stop that man from being your husband if he's meant to be. I'm from Miami, Florida and my husband is from Queens, New York. We come from two very different parts of the country, but the Lord still found a way to bring us to the same place in due season. Let God be God, don't try to do the work for Him and please don't step in and try to manipulate the situation. Don't go making visits to where that man lives or go to church, just to get him to notice you as you walk past him all seductive to get his attention. Don't like each and every one of his posts and pictures on social media so he can get used to seeing your name pop up in his notifications. Chill out, sister! You don't have to do all that, what God has for you is for you.

Many of you know from my story that I've been in this scenario before. There was this one guy I'll refer to as Chico, who I called my "first love" and I really thought he was "the one". Everything played out like a movie or fairytale, but it was all my doing, not God's. The only reason this man ended up recognizing me is because I was determined in my heart to see him again, determined in my heart to have him notice me and I was drawn away by my own lusts. I had enough "faith" to make something happen that wasn't meant to be. Then it all backfired on me. I ended up in a long and detrimental relationship with the guy. He said he wanted to marry me and we could live at his parents' house, which was his plan.

Slowly, my self-induced fairytale turned into a nightmare. I was drawing further away from God than I'd ever been. This man manipulated and verbally abused me. I was fearfully stuck in the relationship because he threatened many times to commit suicide if I left him. I picked up many bad habits in the relationship, such as cursing, because he was a rapper and encouraged me to repeat the lyrics to his favorite songs. I tried weed because he smoked every day and even though I was a virgin, we got into the habit of "sexting" and sending naked pictures, so I definitely wasn't pure.

One night, I remember wanting to break up with him so bad and he felt it. He was sitting on top of a roof while on the phone with me and he told me he'd jump if I broke up with him. I wanted to break up because I could no longer take the disrespect. He changed during our relationship and I suffered the emotional abuse of being called out of my name, being belittled, and controlled. I felt trapped. I felt empty, too.

On the fourth of July before tenth-grade started, I had a breakdown and went into prayer. I cried out to God. I repented for all I had done in the relationship, and I told Him I felt trapped and scared. What I had begun to control was getting out of control. I realized the truth of my doings and that God had nothing to do with it. I asked Him to take Chico out of my life somehow, and I told Him I would dedicate myself to getting to know Him. I went to bed in tears, just hoping God would make a way.

The next morning Chico called and told me he'd had a weird dream. When I asked him what the dream was, he told me it was of us breaking up.

I said, "Maybe this is a sign from God."
He said, "Yeah."

Just like that, we were no longer together. He had agreed so smoothly, I hung up and was at peace. I began my journey at that point; truly building a relationship with God and considering myself saved. Even though I would make mistakes in my next relationship, which was my first engagement, I knew God desired more from me, that He wanted a relationship with me and He wanted me to trust Him to write my love story.

Now, if you honestly feel led by the Holy Spirit to move to that state, the church, school, or wherever it may be where that person is, do it. Be led by the Holy Spirit and step out in faith. But keep in mind that your purpose is far greater than a man. Maybe God is calling you there to set the stage for you and your future spouse but, most likely, He has other things for you to do at that place besides sitting around and waiting for your "Adam" to wake up!

Maybe there's a ministry He wants you to get involved in, some other people He wants you to meet, a book He wants you to write. Don't get so caught up and distracted in waiting on this man that you don't recognize the other areas in which God is trying to work on in your life. You want to be prepared when that time does come and, if anything, you want to make sure you're not prolonging your season. Not doing what the Lord may want you to do or complete before He brings that man around can definitely prolong the process.

Now, back to trusting God. If you're going to trust God, seriously trust God. Meaning, that even if things don't turn out the way you expected, even if somehow, time goes by and the guy ends up marrying someone else and you're sitting around wondering, *what happened, God? Did I hear you wrong?* Know that He is, always has been, and always will be, in control. Don't let minor events, setbacks, or unexpected outcomes break your faith. Instead, use every opportunity to exercise your faith. Faith doesn't say, "This is what I'm expecting to see." Faith says, "I am hoping for the best, because I trust in God, and even though I don't see what's going on…I know whatever He has in store for me is the best." That is why the word in Hebrews 11:1, says,

"Now faith is the substance of things hoped for, the evidence of things not seen."

People take that verse and they think it means: *One day I'm going to see whatever it is I am hoping for.* But that's not fully correct. It means, one day my hope will be fulfilled. God is not trying to meet each and every one of the expectations and requests you throw before Him, but He will fulfill your hope, even if it's not in the way you expect. He is fulfilling your hope, not your idea. So even if your idea does not manifest, your hope shouldn't be lost. You should still have hope because your evidence is not in what you can see, but what you can't see.

PART THREE:

Overcoming the Embarrassment: "I Was Wrong"

"I was wrong. He's with someone else."

The moment of embarrassment...because the person you thought you'd spend the rest of your life with, got married to or is with someone else. What do we do in situations like these? What do we do when the reality that we could've been wrong begins to hit? Many of us will start to think, *"Did I hear God right?"* *"Are they being disobedient?"* or *"Am I just crazy?"* Thoughts like these can take a toll on your mind and on your entire confidence. In that moment, you're not sure of anything and you regret using the phrases, "God said" or "God revealed". How do you recoup when what you thought God promised you doesn't actually come to pass?

How do you cope with the confusing aftermath coming out of this situation and the emotional damage incurred? How do you pick yourself up from such a heavy blow? You just spent months, maybe even years of your life, fantasizing over something not meant to be. During that time, most, if not all of your prayer life was surrounded around this person and from time to time you faced many battles of fear, doubt, confusion, and so on. It's okay to admit you are completely drained and exhausted. You don't even know who you are anymore, you wonder what your life means, and you question your purpose.

Trust me, I know these feelings and I know this experience well, because I've been there. Not just me, but many other women too. You are not alone, and I am here to reassure you that God has dealt with this type of situation before. He knows how to build something new in the place of brokenness and disaster. He heals the brokenhearted and binds their wounds (Psalm 147:3). We have all made mistakes or have been in situations we don't understand. Know for all of the mistakes and for all of those situations, God can and will show Himself sovereign and glorious if we continue to seek Him.

In this chapter, I want to focus on how to cope with the fact you were wrong and give tips and encouragement on moving forward. Sis, the first step to moving on and healing from the process is acceptance. As much as you are tempted to blame the other person or blame God, you just can't. If you go on the rest of your life telling yourself the person you were supposed to be with was disobedient to God, filled with lust, and not spending enough time in prayer to marry you, you will grow bitter, restless, and feel anger and resentment towards couples and relationships that do work out. You will get used to pointing the finger at others, saying things like, "Pshhh, I doubt that relationship will last long, he's probably cheating," or "Everyone wants to be married, look at all the couples everywhere. Why can't people just be content? I'm content." Check your heart. That bitter seed is not doing you any good and will just make you more and more miserable every single day that passes by. It will make you jealous and envious of everyone's relationship when the truth is, you're just really heartbroken, you're just really angry. You internalized the situation by blaming everyone around you and you never allowed your process of healing to take place.

If this is you, I challenge you to close the door you allowed the enemy to have in your life. He doesn't want you to be happy. He wants you to remain down in the dumps, he wants you to be sad, feel like there's no hope for your life, and have you think, *"When is my time, God?"* and *"There are no good men out there."* Repent; let go of any offense you have towards that person, pray for them. Pray they are in God's will and they are happy in their new relationship… pray their new relationship is God glorifying and purpose-filled. God has not forgotten about you, your time will come.

Remember, don't blame God either. You have to understand God does not lie. He would not and He could not because He is holy. You also need to learn how to trust Him in the midst of all your chaos. He is not the cause of your chaos, but even in the midst of the storm, He will be with you. Don't blame God for the confusing season you are in, it is not His fault and He is not trying to confuse us. God is the author of peace. Our confusion is our own and it's up to us to run to Him for peace.

We get confused when we are constantly tempted by the devil, and we aren't properly equipped to fight back. Confusion happens in the mind, and if you are constantly losing in the battlefield of your mind, the result is chaos. We need to accept that we must start winning battles and start making the right turns so we don't keep ending up at dead ends. When we don't put on the armor of God and when we let our minds be controlled by our emotions, feelings, and fantasies, we set ourselves up for failure.

Accept the fact that you are in a confusing situation, but don't blame God for it. We don't have to come to God as if we know everything; He knows we don't. You don't have to understand and figure out why it happened in order to move on and be at peace. Peace does not come from thinking we have everything figured out, because once we think we have everything figured out, life will throw us another curve ball. Peace comes from humbling ourselves and trusting God. The bible says,

"Do not be anxious about anything, but in every situation, by prayer and petition, with thanksgiving, present your requests to God. And the peace of God, which transcends all understanding, will guard your hearts and your minds in Christ Jesus." - Philippians 4:6-7

If this is you, and you feel led, repeat this prayer:

Daddy, I am so embarrassed. I thought I heard you right but I missed it somehow. Lord, please forgive me. I know it is not Your fault, and I know You would never do anything to hurt me. You love me, Lord, and I know your plans for me are great. You are a faithful God and You will establish and complete the work You began in me and in my heart. Father, I forgive anyone who may have hurt me throughout this process. I let go of my feelings of resentment, hatred, and jealousy now. Lord, though I do not understand, please give me the strength and patience to trust You with my entire life. I thank You so much, Lord, for all You have in store, and for all You are. In Jesus' name I pray, Amen.

"My clock is ticking – you don't understand"

Even though I shared the experiences of my single season, you may still say, "Karolyne, you don't understand. You're married now. My biological clock is ticking and I've been single longer. It's easy for you to preach to me."

You know what? Maybe your season is different, and the process may even be tougher than what I had to endure. With that being said, I've decided to pull the testimony of a woman I met a little while ago. Her testimony impacted me so much when I first heard it; I decided to conduct an official interview with her to be able to share it with you. This woman goes by the name of Arminta Elias. Below are excerpts from the written interview in addition to my questions and her responses. I hope you are just as blessed as I was from hearing her story and how she overcame a great hardship and tragedy during her season of singleness. She is still single, in expectation for God's best. If you can't relate to me or anything else I've written in this book, Arminta is very relatable.

-- Recorded Interview --

Karolyne Roberts:

"Hello Arminta, I am meeting with you today because I believe you have a very powerful testimony as it pertains to your experience during singleness, and you are very relatable. I know we've spoken about your story before, but for the singles reading my book unaware of your story, do you mind sharing the experience you faced, which we spoke about previously?"

Arminta Elias:

"Back in Sept 15, 2012, I was forced to walk into a place full of family and friends and marry a man who was never going to show up. I was told I had to walk by faith and trust God. (Can you imagine what that felt like and how hard it was for me to trust God? Even now!)

I never planned to marry the man. As a matter of fact, we had broken up mutually in February 2012 and I decided to become celibate and seek God. I had no plans on marrying no man at the moment. I wasn't dating and there was no man in sight. But the church I was attending, the pastor had told me my husband was the very young man I had just broken up with. To be honest, I didn't want to marry him because he cheated on me in the relationship and I wanted to start fresh and leave the past in the past and I was fine without him. I was at peace with the break up.

The pastor told me to start planning the wedding, and I did. But in the back of my mind, I didn't feel comfortable. Why would God want me to marry someone I don't feel comfortable marrying? But she was my pastor and I was just learning. I had no knowledge of the Bible or the principles. I was seeking to know God and that's how I got sucked in.

Well, fast forward to Sept 2012. I called the young man and said I was told that we have to get married and he said, "I'm not marrying you." I told the pastor and she said, "Trust God." I was like, okay, but I was confused. (So messed up!) On the day of the wedding, I was up at eight o'clock to go get my dress. Even then I just knew this was crazy and insane, but I had told all these people and there were gifts and people were bringing dishes. It was a catastrophe!

The whole ride to look for the dress I had a pounding headache and I was so nervous and so freaked out because I knew this couldn't be happening. I called my pastor after I got the dress and I told her I didn't want to marry him and I didn't want to go through with it and she told me, "If you don't go through with this, you cannot be a part of our ministry or church." That was hurtful. I felt a piercing in my heart. Like who would make someone do something so crazy?

I arrived at the pavilion and I was dolled up in a beautiful white gown with a veil and my mom put my jewelry on and I looked gorgeous, but inside I felt horrible. I walked into a place full of people asking, where is the groom? Is he late? Have you talked to him? All I could say was, "He should be on his way." But I knew he wasn't coming. I stood in front of all these people for thirty minutes and I looked at everyone with tears in my eyes and I said, "I don't think he's coming." I felt my heart drop to the pit of my stomach. All I could do was sit. My head was spinning and I had no idea what was going on.

The people still stayed and ate with me, but it hurt to know all along that no man was coming and I was the butt of the joke. After everyone had cleared out, my pastor drove me home and she said, "You were healed today. I am proud of you. God is proud of you and your faith." And she smiled, but I wasn't smiling. I was angry. I was hurt. I was sad. I was mad at God!

How could You do this to me? How could You embarrass and shame me in front of all of those people and then say You love me and to trust You?

From that moment on, I didn't trust God. I didn't trust anything prophesied over my life. I didn't trust anything to do with God. I was going to church, but I wasn't getting anything. I was bottling up all the hurt, shame, embarrassment and pain on the inside.

I felt as if God was out to trick or punish me or make a fool of me. I didn't get the healing I needed until I admitted to God that I didn't trust Him and I didn't want to because of what He had allowed. "I didn't know any better. I was just being obedient and You allowed that to happen to me. How can I trust You?" I shouted at God.

But when I did that, I experienced God for the first time; He wouldn't do that to me. That wasn't of Him. I was misused, manipulated, abused and His name was used, but it wasn't of Him. It was at the new church I joined in April 2013 where I received the healing and I begin to develop a relationship with God."

Karolyne Roberts:

"Do you blame yourself for any part of what happened? Being that you had knowledge of the truth?"

Arminta Elias:

"I do blame myself because I felt as though I should've followed my instinct and I should've turned it down."

Karolyne Roberts:

"Deep down inside, did you want it to be true?"

Arminta Elias:

"Deep down I wanted him to show up so it didn't seem real that it wasn't true."

Karolyne Roberts:

"What inspired you and gave you the courage to finally come out and share your testimony?"

Arminta Elias:

"When I joined the new church, after a prayer meeting, I shared the story with some and I had still had the wedding dress and veil and wedding band and I really felt as though I needed to get rid of it in order to move on from the hurt."

Karolyne Roberts:

"How has this experience changed you and shifted your view on both marriage and singleness?"

Arminta Elias:

"The experience, though it hurt, helped. It helped me be steadfast in my singleness and it drew me closer to God and to learn of what true singleness is and the struggles and the traps out there. As far as marriage, it has helped me realize marriage is more than a pretty, white dress and a roomful of people and gifts. Marriage is ministry and if you really read on the marriages in the Old Testament, you will see how marriage has been misconstrued and taken out of context. Most young ladies are more fascinated with the proposal and the wedding day, they don't consider it's for eternity and that God has work for you to do within it."

Karolyne Roberts:

"What would you tell other women who have faced embarrassment from situations like yours?"

Arminta Elias:

"I wouldn't want that to happen to anyone, but I will say that God doesn't do bad things to us. However, God does allow things to happen to us and as crazy as it may seem and though you don't understand—know that if marriage seems hard for you to accomplish, it's because the enemy knows there's purpose in it.

I used to say if getting married is this difficult, I don't want it. But the enemy only attacks what God has ordained and there's a purpose in it. Just be patient and let God choose for you."

Karolyne Roberts:

"Why do you think you desired the approval of your Pastor and being accepted into the ministry bad enough to follow through with that?"

Arminta Elias:

"I felt like I belonged to something. She was nice and she made me feel accepted. She would tell me all these great things God had for me; feeding my self-esteem and my ego. I didn't know who I was and I didn't know anything about God so I was "fresh meat".

I had been in multiple relationships, all kinds of relationships, nothing was going well in my life and I figured this church was a great place for me."

Karolyne Roberts:

"How would you recommend other single women or women in general, to beware and recognize these manipulative types of people?"

Arminta Elias:

"I would say, even though we don't have the relationship with God we desire or we think we should have, God still speaks to us and He still moves in our lives. I believe a lot of times we see our leaders as hearing from God better and more than we do, so we chalk up what God is telling us as our imagination and though it feels wrong and we know we shouldn't heed it, we still do because we don't have faith that God loves us and speaks to us just as He does everyone else."

Karolyne Roberts:

"How old are you? And have you ever struggled with discontentment for still being single at your age? What are some struggles you've faced?"

Arminta Elias:

"As a single parent, you wonder if your child will be accepted and received. Being over thirty and single has also been a struggle because many people find this funny, especially family. My mom would question me repeatedly as to when I was getting married because my time was ticking and my son is seven years old and he needs siblings.

Contentment was a big problem of mine. It was hard to "be still". I used to say it's easier said than done when you're engaged to be married or already married or playing house, but when you truly want to please God and you're doing everything God is asking and you're still not seeing any progress, it's hard to be content. It seems like everyone is compromising and getting further than you are and if you're not careful, you'll think about compromising, too!"

Karolyne Roberts:

"What methods have you used to battle feelings of discontentment? Which methods worked? And which methods failed?"

Arminta Elias:

"For a long time I tried to smooth over what was really bothering me as if I wasn't bothered at all but I was. At the end of the day, I didn't want to be single. I wanted to be loved and I wanted to give love. I wanted to have a family and to enjoy the goodness of Jesus and I honestly felt He would give me that. And then of course I had urges. Try telling someone that and watch what happens.

I remember asking God to "take away the urges" because I felt like I was a bad person, but no one wanted to talk about it, they just wanted to rebuke you and say it was a lustful demon when it's natural! Especially to women who have been exposed to it.

So those were feelings I couldn't open up about because I was told I needed to be delivered from a "lust demon".

To be honest, the only method is talking about it, getting to the root of it and being open and honest with God. Once you do that, God can deal with you and show you how to deal with it."

Karolyne Roberts:

"Overall, what have you learned from this situation?"

Arminta Elias:

"I have learned to be more open to others and be open to God because, though we think we have God figured out, we really don't and you can limit yourself to what God wants to do in your life because of your mentality. Also, do not give so much credit to Satan. Granted, he does attack, but I've found myself giving him so much that I lived in fear and suspicion when God tells me something and I can barely enjoy it because I'm afraid of the devil."

God will talk to you on your level. Remember that! I use to think talking with God was like the way the Bible is written,

"Thee, thou, etc." but God talks to me just as you and I are talking—plain and clear and with clarity.

Also, don't overindulge in too much material; it can dilute what God is telling you. I know from experience. God wants to speak to you, but when you have the "speaking" of others in your mind and their thoughts, you can confuse them with what God is telling you.

I enjoy reading and following inspirational speakers, but I became dependent on Joyce Meyer and Joel Osteen and Jesse Duplantis to the point where their words clouded what God was giving me. I had to know when to put the book down and read His word and hear Him for myself. Lastly, be careful of seeking too much confirmation, that's an open door for the enemy."

-- End of Interview –

I think we can learn a lot from Arminta's testimony and many of the insights she shared. A lot of times, our focus is on our biological clock versus God's timing because the people and all the voices around us are telling us we need to be at the next stage and that something is wrong with us. Then, when we finally do get to that next stage, it's the next thing, then the next thing. We are never satisfied and fully able to enjoy each season because we let these people's opinions and pressures rule our lives. If we keep looking to men to approve of our season, we will never find joy in this life. God did not intend for you to go through life miserable, even when you do face rough seasons, you can have joy.

"I know what it is to be in need, and I know what it is to have plenty. I have learned the secret of being content in any and every situation, whether well fed or hungry, whether living in plenty or in want." - Philippians 4:12

I love how Paul calls this a "secret" because even though contentment is widely talked about nowadays, especially when it comes to singlehood, I don't think people realize how much of a golden nugget and gift it is. The ability to be content comes from God...because we have a hope that surpasses our current situation. We can be content when we take our focus off of "now" and have eternity in mind.

I know how it feels to be embarrassed, I know how it feels to be discouraged and let down when you thought something was going to happen, or when you were looking forward to spending the rest of your life with that person. I have had those moments. I thought my first engagement would last and turn into a beautiful and fulfilling marriage, but finding out my ex cheated on me was not only devastating, but embarrassing because it was with his "best friend" and I should've know better.

I was deceived, but God was still able to heal my wounds and heal my hurt when I felt lonely. I was able to find joy in contentment when I felt like no one else understood. God understood. God saw, even if I couldn't relate to everyone in my situation. Even though people around me may have deemed my situation or my circumstance as hopeless, I still clung to the hope that no man could take away from me, and you can, too.

Our Final Hope

Now, if you've gotten to this point after reading the book and still believe God has revealed who your husband is, stay encouraged. God always fulfills His promises. If you have not seen the fruit of that promise yet, it will still come to pass. Take the story of Abraham for example. In Genesis 17: 1-7 it says:

> "Abram was ninety-nine years old when the Lord appeared to him again and said, "I am God All-Powerful. If you obey me and always do right, I will keep my solemn promise to you and give you more descendants than can be counted." Abram bowed with his face to the ground, and God said:
>
> I promise that you will be the father of many nations. That's why I now change your name from Abram to Abraham. I will give you a lot of descendants, and in the future they will become great nations. Some of them will even be kings.
>
> I will always keep the promise I have made to you and your descendants, because I am your God and their God. I will give you and them the land in which you are now a foreigner. I will give the whole land of

Canaan to your family forever, and I will be their God"

God kept His promise to Abraham. Can you believe we ourselves are descendants of Abraham and God promised us to him? He is not even here to witness the fruit of the promise, but the promise is still fulfilled to this day. Then, if we keep reading verses 17-21, it says:

> Abraham bowed with his face to the ground and thought, "I am almost a hundred years old. How can I become a father? And Sarah is ninety. How can she have a child?" So he started laughing. Then he asked God, "Why not let Ishmael inherit what you have promised me?"

> But God answered: No! You and Sarah will have a son. His name will be Isaac and I will make an everlasting promise to him and his descendants.

> I have heard what you asked me to do for Ishmael, and so I will also bless him with many descendants. He will be the father of twelve princes, and I will make his family a great nation. But your son Isaac will be born about this time next year, and the

promise I am making to you and your family will be for him and his descendants forever.

You may be like Abraham. You may think, *I am thirty plus years old already. Will God still keep His promise? Will I still end up marrying this man? My clock is ticking.* Abraham was almost one hundred years old! You may be tempted, like Abraham, to create an Ishmael (an answer to what you believe is a problem) even though it's not God's will. If God promised you something, it's your job to continue in faith that one day, the promise will be fulfilled. It's not your job to look at all the reasons why the promise seems impossible, and try to present an Ishmael to pacify your impatience and fear in the situation. God wants to give you an Isaac. Are you willing to wait on Him and trust Him? Abraham was able to see Isaac born as God promised, in his lifetime.

The thing about the promise is that we can't idolize God's promise over Him. We should want God *more* than His promises. He is our answered prayer, before we could even ask. Even with God fulfilling His promise of Chris being the man I would marry during this lifetime, this is not the end. There is a greater promise that awaits me... the promise of the return of my King, my Lord, and Savior, Jesus Christ.

My soul longs for the day I will see Him standing before me, in His incomparable beauty, strength, and majesty, and then I will be, forever satisfied...

"One thing I ask from the LORD, this only do I seek: that I may dwell in the house of the LORD all the days of my life, to gaze on the beauty of the LORD and to seek him in his temple." – Psalm 27:4

About the Author

Karolyne Roberts is the wife to Christopher Roberts, mother, author, worshipper, and entrepreneur. She is a young and talented spiritual powerhouse, dedicated to spreading God's love to the masses.

Karolyne is the Founder and CEO of a publishing company called IAMIMAGE, which is committed to helping new Christian authors establish their voice and share their testimony—all for the glory of God! She is also a Christian lifestyle vlogger alongside her husband, Chris, on TheRobertsLive.Com. Together, they share the ins and outs and ups and downs of their perfectly imperfect lives.

So far, Karolyne has penned three books, "Before Saying 'Yes' to the Ring", "Young and Living for God", and "The One" Revealed. In her spare time she runs a blog that addresses multiple topics relating to purpose, relationships, spiritual warfare, and more. Karolyne utilizes her gift of writing to reach the masses through many different outlets. Her spoken word poetry has made its stamp in the Christian community as well as the general public and her blog has attracted readers from all over the world.

Outside of writing, vlogging, and being a family woman, Karolyne recognizes worship and spoken word as an integral part of her expression to God and evangelism to others. She seeks to continually lead God's people into a true encounter with His presence as she lives this out on a day-to-day basis.

Check out Karolyne's work:

www. IAMIMAGE.com

www.KarolyneRoberts.com

Connect with Karolyne on social media:

FACEBOOK: Karolyne Roberts

INSTAGRAM:
http://www.instagram.com/KarolyneRoberts

YOUTUBE: http://www. youtube.com/KarolyneRoberts

YOUTUBE: http://www.youtube.com/TheRobertsLive

TWITTER: http://www. twiter.com/KarolyneRoberts

PINTEREST: http://www. pinterest.com/KarolyneRoberts

PERISCOPE: Karolyne Roberts

Notes

_____

_____

_____

_____

_____

_____

_____

_____